SOCIAL GEOGRAPHIES

THE BASICS

Social Geographies: The Basics introduces what social geography is, and what it might be. It outlines the key contours of social geographies, and also disrupts some of the conventions of the discipline in both its content and structure.

This book approaches social geographies by beginning with the resistances, contestations and 'solutions' that communities use to challenge exclusions in place and space in order to create equitable societies. It then addresses the inequalities, precarities, and 'problems' that prompt these interventions. This allows the book to emphasise the importance of activism in the here and now, and to show how activism often makes issues visible and contested in ways that are then theorised by academics. *Social Geographies* starts with solidarities, communities, and networks before moving to examine difference, precarity, and mobilities. Each chapter offers key case studies that centre resistance, contestations of inequitable power, and local knowledges that can often be seen as 'solutions' to national and transnational issues, creating a decolonial understanding of 'social geography from below' within and across national contexts.

This book is essential reading for undergraduate students and readers new to the area, as well as anyone studying introductory geography, social, cultural and critical geography, 'the spatial turn' and issues of spatialities, and key issues like precarity, power, difference, equality, and mobilities.

Kath Browne is Professor of Geography at University College Dublin, Ireland. Her research focuses on social justice and inequalities, specifically around gender and sexualities. She has worked with those marginalised because of their sexual and gender identities, exploring how lives can be ameliorated in ways that take place seriously. She has also worked on those who are opposed to sexual and gender equalities, developing the concept of heteroactivism. She leads the Beyond Opposition research project.

Dhiren Borisa is a Dalit queer activist, poet and urban sexual geographer and is Assistant Professor at Jindal Global Law School, India. He is an Urban Studies International Fellow 2022. Dhiren attained his PhD from Jawaharlal Nehru University, New Delhi on queer cartographies of desires in Delhi. His research engages with sexual mappings and makings of cities from an intersectional and decolonial lens both among queer spaces in India and in diasporic queer worldings.

Mary Gilmartin is Professor of Geography at Maynooth University, Ireland. Her research focuses on migration, mobilities and spatial justice, and she has extensive experience of teaching undergraduate courses in social geography. She was Managing Editor of the journal *Social & Cultural Geography* from 2014 to 2018, and remains a member of that journal's editorial board.

Niharika Banerjea teaches gender sexuality and queer studies at the Jindal Global Law School, O.P. Jindal Global University, India. Working across and drawing from sociology, geographies of sexualities, and social anthropology, she is engaged with queer-feminist living and activisms in contemporary India. She identifies as a queer academic activist as a way to critically address familiar binaries between academia and activism – in classrooms, activist spaces, and writing practices. Niharika is a member of Sappho for Equality, the activist forum for lesbian, bisexual women, and transmasculine persons' rights.

The Basics Series

The Basics is a highly successful series of accessible guidebooks which provide an overview of the fundamental principles of a subject area in a jargon-free and undaunting format.

Intended for students approaching a subject for the first time, the books both introduce the essentials of a subject and provide an ideal springboard for further study. With over 50 titles spanning subjects from artificial intelligence (AI) to women's studies, *The Basics* are an ideal starting point for students seeking to understand a subject area.

Each text comes with recommendations for further study and gradually introduces the complexities and nuances within a subject.

EATING DISORDERS
ELIZABETH MCNAUGHT, JANET TREASURE, AND JESS GRIFFITHS

TRUTH
JC BEALL AND BEN MIDDLETON

PERCEPTION
BENCE NANAY

C.G. JUNG'S COLLECTED WORKS
ANN YEOMAN AND KEVIN LU

CORPORATE FINANCE
TERENCE C.M. TSE

FILM GENRE
BARRY KEITH GRANT

RELIGIONS AND SPORTS
TERRY D. SHOEMAKER

CRITICAL THEORY
MARTIN SHUSTER

SOCIAL GEOGRAPHIES
KATH BROWNE, DHIREN BORISA, MARY GILMARTIN, AND NIHARIKA BANERJEA

JAPAN (SECOND EDITION)
CHRISTOPHER P. HOOD

For a full list of titles in this series, please visit www.routledge.com/ The-Basics/book-series/B

SOCIAL GEOGRAPHIES
THE BASICS

Kath Browne, Dhiren Borisa,
Mary Gilmartin, and Niharika Banerjea

LONDON AND NEW YORK

Designed cover image: PeterAustin/Getty Images

First published 2024
by Routledge
4 Park Square, Milton Park, Abingdon, Oxon OX14 4RN

and by Routledge
605 Third Avenue, New York, NY 10158

Routledge is an imprint of the Taylor & Francis Group, an informa business

© 2024 Kath Browne, Dhiren Borisa, Mary Gilmartin and Niharika Banerjea

The right of Kath Browne, Dhiren Borisa, Mary Gilmartin and Niharika Banerjea to be identified as authors of this work has been asserted in accordance with sections 77 and 78 of the Copyright, Designs and Patents Act 1988.

All rights reserved. No part of this book may be reprinted or reproduced or utilised in any form or by any electronic, mechanical, or other means, now known or hereafter invented, including photocopying and recording, or in any information storage or retrieval system, without permission in writing from the publishers.

Trademark notice: Product or corporate names may be trademarks or registered trademarks, and are used only for identification and explanation without intent to infringe.

British Library Cataloguing-in-Publication Data
A catalogue record for this book is available from the British Library

Library of Congress Cataloging-in-Publication Data
Names: Browne, Kath, author. | Borisa, Dhiren, author. |
    Gilmartin, Mary, 1969–author. | Banerjea, Niharika, author.
Title: Social geographies : the basics / Kath Browne, Dhiren Borisa,
    Mary Gilmartin and Niharika Banerjea.
Description: Abingdon, Oxon ; New York, NY : Routledge, 2024. |
    Includes bibliographical references and index. |
Identifiers: LCCN 2023050255 | ISBN 9781032201832 (hardback) |
    ISBN 9781032211251 (paperback) | ISBN 9781003266877 (ebook)
Subjects: LCSH: Human geography.
Classification: LCC GF41 .B779 2024 | DDC 304.2—dc23/eng/20231201
LC record available at https://lccn.loc.gov/2023050255

ISBN: 978-1-032-20183-2 (hbk)
ISBN: 978-1-032-21125-1 (pbk)
ISBN: 978-1-003-26687-7 (ebk)

DOI: 10.4324/9781003266877

Typeset in Bembo
by Apex CoVantage, LLC

CONTENTS

List of figures	viii
Acknowledgements	x
Introduction: defining social geographies	1
1 **Making social change possible: communities, activism, resistance, and solidarity**	33
2 **Geographies of difference**	63
3 **Geographies of precarity**	92
4 **Movement, migration, mobilities**	124
Conclusion: concluding dialogue	153
References	178
Index	184

FIGURES

0.1	Peet's Schools of Modern and Postmodern Geographical Thought.	9
1.1	Collage of the Arab Spring.	35
1.2	Protest against Vedanta Corporation.	39
1.3	Repeal Campaigners in Dublin North-West, 2018.	44
1.4	Temporary Memorial to Savita Halappanavar in Dublin, May 2018.	46
1.5	Farmers' Union Protest, India 2020.	50
1.6	Farmers' Protest at Delhi's Tikri Border, 2020.	51
1.7	BLM Graffitied Wall in Harlem NY, US.	54
1.8	#DalitWomenFight Protest at the Dalit Women Fight Yatra in the US, 2015.	58
2.1	Photo of McDonalds in New Delhi, India.	66
2.2	Photo of The Irish House, Indira Gandhi International Airport, New Delhi, India on 14 February 2023.	67
2.3	Bunge's Map of Detroit 'Rat Bitten Babies' 1975.	71
2.4	Photo of Gated Communities in Dublin, Ireland.	77
2.5	Photo of DART Benches in Dublin, Ireland.	79
2.6	Photo of Clothes Labels.	85

FIGURES ix

2.7	Photo of Traffic Signals, Leicester City Railway Station on 24 February 2023.	88
3.1	Protest against Niqab/Burqa Ban in Copenhagen, Denmark, 2018.	100
3.2	Protests in Shaheen Bagh, New Delhi, India.	102
3.3	Gig Economy Strikers in Italy.	111
3.4	Delhi Pride March, Map and Photo.	115
3.5	Sandeep Nagar Dairy Farm, Tamil Nadu, India.	120
4.1	Stranded Migrant Workers during COVID-19 Lockdown, India 2020.	127
4.2	Shenzhen North Railway Station during Chungun, 2016.	132
4.3	Steep Slope Warning Sign in Dublin, Ireland.	141
5.1	Drawing Representing Zoom Call Dialogue among Authors on Possible Social Geographies.	154

ACKNOWLEDGEMENTS

The authors would like to thank all those who have built social geographies into the diverse area that it is impossible to encapsulate in this book.

We would like to thank Jason Roche who read an early version of the book and gave us interesting ideas and insights from an undergraduate perspective. Thanks to Maynooth University's summer internship programme for supporting this work. Thanks to MKF for their work on the final drafts, and thanks to Prateek Draik, Karen Fagan, Aoife Fox, and Richard Peet for providing images. We would also like to thank Grace Banu, Jacinta Kerketta, Sukirtha Rani, Urmila, and Dhrubo Jyoti for generously allowing us to use their poetry and creative interventions and for making lives loveable and liveable for all of us despite all that stops us from being.

Thanks to Andrew Mould and all at Routledge for the initial approach about a book in this area, and for their support (and patience!) in delivering this manuscript.

INTRODUCTION
Defining social geographies

I. INTRODUCTION

Our world is in disarray. We can see this in so many ways, from the climate crisis that threatens the future of our planet to the economic and social inequalities that make some lives seem less important and valuable than others, to the growth in authoritarian regimes that seek to impose restrictions on the lives and practices of marginalised peoples. We face different challenges depending on where we live and who we are. For some of us, water shortages may be the most pressing issue that we face each day. For others, the cost of living may make it difficult for us to live decent lives. Some of us may identify in a way that is not easily accepted in our homes, such as when we identify within the LGBTQI+ spectrum. Others may be part of a racial or ethnic minority, experiencing both structural and everyday racism. Still others may be part of oppressed caste groups, facing overt and covert forms of discrimination in public and private spaces. However, we don't want you to feel despair at the thought of all these challenges. Consider, instead, how we might come together to face the challenges that confront us and bring about positive change. This brings us to social geography, which is the subject matter of this book.

WHAT IS SOCIAL GEOGRAPHY?

This seems like an easy question to answer, but the meaning of social geography has been contested and changed over time. In social geography, like all other academic disciplines, how we define social geography

DOI: 10.4324/9781003266877-1

depends on our perspective on knowledge creation. One perspective says that social geography is best defined by the key thinkers: the important people who have shaped our understanding of the discipline. Another perspective says that social geography is best defined by the key texts on the topic: the books that are widely read and critically valued. Yet another perspective says that social geography is best defined through practice: by the work done by people who call themselves or are identified as social geographers. Because of this, there is no easy definition of 'social geography'. This is not a new issue. Writing in 1968, the geographer Anne Buttimer claimed that "no generally accepted definition of social geography exists",[1] and her observation is as true now as it was when she wrote it.

That said, it's important to first explain how we, the authors of this book, understand social geography. We see 'social' as relating to people, their interactions, and their interconnections: these interactions and interconnections can be between individuals, groups, or with the social structures that people establish and maintain. We see 'geography' as concerned with the world we live in. For us, then, social geography refers to social lives that are made in space and place, and that in turn shape the spaces and places where they exist. As a group of academics, we wrote this book because we believe that to address the inequalities and injustices that we see around us locally, regionally, nationally, and transnationally, we must understand them. We will demonstrate that this can't be done without considering *who* we are and *where* we are. As we inhabit and produce socially stratified geographies through social-spatial practices and relations, what patterns emerge, and can these be disrupted and redrawn to create better possible worlds? Our approach to social geography is based on a concern with bringing about change. We want this to be a hopeful book, highlighting the ideas and tools that social geographers, including you, can use to build a better world.

HOW DOES OUR UNDERSTANDING OF SOCIAL GEOGRAPHY COMPARE TO OTHERS?

We thought it would be helpful to share other definitions so you could see the similarities and differences. A starting point for people learning about geography, in general, is the variety of dictionaries and encyclopedias that aim to provide concise and accessible

INTRODUCTION   3

definitions (Box 0.1). Textbooks also provide definitions of social geography, though these are typically less concise (Box 0.2).

BOX 0.1 DICTIONARY DEFINITIONS

The *Dictionary of Human Geography* defines social geography as "The study of social relations, social identities, and social inequalities from a spatial perspective".[2] The *International Encyclopedia of Geography* defines social geography as "the relationship between society and space, with a particular emphasis on issues related to social identity, nature, relevance, and justice".[3]

BOX 0.2 TEXTBOOK DEFINITIONS

Aijazuddin Ahmed in 1999 published the first textbook in social geography from India based on 24 years of teaching in this area. He defined social geography of India as understanding "social matrix and its politico-geographical interpretation which could facilitate an understanding of social phenomena that defined India – an understanding of diversities – within the larger framework of oneness that formed the basis of the Indian state".[4]

In 2001, Pain et al. described social geography as "concerned with the ways in which social relations, social identities and social inequalities are produced, their spatial variation, and the role of space in constructing them".[5] In the same year, Valentine wrote that "[s]ocial geography is an inherently ambiguous and eclectic field of research and writing. It is perhaps best summed up as 'the study of social relations and the spatial structures that underpin those relations' (Johnston et al., 2000: 753)".[6]

For Panelli, writing in 2004, social geography "is a body of knowledge and a set of practices by which scholars look at, and seek to understand, the social world". Importantly, Panelli saw social geography as giving us "the chance to ask questions, construct explanations – and discover yet more questions – about where and how social differences and interaction occur".[7]

Del Casino, in 2009, described social geography as "a constellation of theoretical and methodological approaches that converge and diverge in an attempt to understand and explain the spatial organization of what we could broadly think of as difference and inequality".[8] In 2010 Smith et al. named the "label of social geography" as: "concerned with the way space mediates the production and reproduction of key social divides [and] the study of social relations and the spatial structures that underpin those relations".[9] Del Casino et al. (2011: 3) defined social geography as "a broad field that attends to the socio-spatial differences, power relations, and inequalities that shape every person's life. Social Geography is also a way of going about the intellectual work that focuses on these very political questions and issues."[10]

Most recently, in 2021, the Newcastle Social Geographies collective described social geography as "the study of the interrelationships between society and space . . . [where] society and space are considered to have a co-constitutive relationship".[11]

There are some similarities between the definitions that indicate patterns that social geographers agree on. These include:

1   Many of these definitions highlight both *society and space*.
2   They are concerned with social groups and their interactions, and how these are influenced by space.
3   There's a particular interest in issues of equality and justice – or, rather, inequalities and injustices – and how these are made by, and make, place.

However, there's much less attention to how the social affects space or place. This is the key difference in our textbook. We will explicitly discuss how the social, including specific social groups such as racialised people, affects and changes space and place.

We also use the plural term social geographies. This is because we don't think that there is one form of social geography. We think there are many, they are different from each other and although we cannot cover everything in one textbook, we highlight the multiple ways that social geographies are thought of, thought through, and practised.

II. LOCATING SOCIAL GEOGRAPHIES: AN 'OFFICIAL' HISTORY

There are different ways in which the story of an academic discipline, like social geography, is constructed and told. This can be through an emphasis on important and famous people, on key texts, or on what the academics do. Some of these approaches will overlap: key thinkers often write important texts, for example, or influence how the discipline is practised. However, what tends to happen is that academic disciplines get defined by and through a small number of people, located in previously or currently powerful countries such as Britain or the United States. As a consequence, the official histories of academic disciplines, like social geography, are located in particular places and they are partial and incomplete. Our overview of the history of social geography is also partial. We highlight key people, key moments, and key ideas as they have been recounted by a variety of people who have charted the development of social geography. We then challenge these stories by looking at critiques that are perhaps less familiar. Critiques that exist alongside the official version are many and we select only a few. These are sometimes called decolonial, which means a version that challenges the dominant narratives that come from colonial powers.

Many of the histories of social geography start in the nineteenth century, with European thinkers and activists. Some of the names who are part of the official history of, Geography, such as Friedrich Ratzel, Paul Vidal de la Blache and Élisée Reclus, are often credited with influencing the development of social geography, though from very different perspectives. Ratzel, based in Germany, wrote several influential books that considered the relationship between the physical environment and people's behaviour. Vidal de la Blache, a French contemporary of Ratzel, also considered the relationship between environment and human institutions: he called this *les genres de vie*, translated as 'the patterns of living'. A third contemporary was Élisée Reclus, born in France and often described as an anarchist and geographer. It's been claimed that he was the first geographer to use the term 'social geography', though he didn't formally define it.[12] Though these three geographers had different political positions and reached different conclusions,

INTRODUCTION

their main focus was the relationship between environment and society – both broadly defined.

Geographers such as Ratzel, Vidal de la Blache and Reclus provided inspiration for the definition and development of social geography within the discipline of Geography. Inspiration also came from others, particularly the work of urban sociologists known as the Chicago School, working in the early twentieth century. Based at the University of Chicago, these scholars sought to use ethnographic approaches – that is, observing people in the spaces where they are – to better understand the significant changes that were happening in the city of Chicago, as it grew rapidly through internal and international migration. Chicago School academics and associates, such as Robert Park, Ernest Burgess, and Jane Addams, are important figures in urban studies. They are also important figures in social geography because they moved the focus of social geography from the rural areas that were studied by people like Vidal de la Blache to urban areas. Consequently, social geography has long had a particular emphasis on cities, perhaps because cities offer a concentration of diverse people, which in turn means differences and the presence of inequalities. Therefore, cities tend to offer a more visible demonstration of social inequalities and power relations, and often are places where social groups gather to protest, create communities, and make change.

Different approaches to social geography developed in different countries, such as France, Germany, the Netherlands, the UK, and the US, at different times. However, social geography across a range of national contexts was profoundly influenced by several different events from the 1960s onwards. The first was the range of social movements that emerged, worldwide: student movements, feminism, anti-war movements, challenges to racism, anti-imperialism, gay liberation, and environmentalism. These varied social movements challenged academic disciplines, like Geography, to be more socially relevant. The second was the influence of Marxism on social geography[13] (Box 0.3). The geographer David Harvey played a very important role in developing Marxist thought in Geography, and in social geography. His 1973 book, *Social Justice and the City*, was his first sustained effort to consider the development and function of cities from a Marxist perspective. Harvey describes his book as concerned with the relationship between "social process and spatial

INTRODUCTION   7

form"; he thought this could be clearly shown in cities, and that cities could also be appropriate sites for a "revolutionary theory" that imagined an alternative to capitalism.[14] Harvey's work has been very influential within and beyond social geography because of its theoretical coherence, its urban focus, and its normative orientation. Much work in social geography and beyond in anti-capitalist work, around the world, has drawn inspiration from David Harvey and from Marxism, and has focused on inequalities, injustices, and on ways of remaking cities as better places for a diverse set of people.

> ### BOX 0.3 MARXISM
>
> An approach to understanding the world derived from the work of Karl Marx. Marxism is particularly concerned with explaining how our world is shaped by capitalism as an economic and political system, and with providing alternatives to capitalism that are more just and less exploitative.

While social geography was becoming influenced by Marxism, it was also being challenged by other developments in human geography. The 'cultural turn' in geography was a reaction against traditional approaches to cultural geography, which were seen as atheoretical and descriptive, conservative, and overly concerned with rural areas (Box 0.4). The concerns of this 'new cultural geography' including with power, difference and inequalities so overlapped with social geography that they started to be thought of as similar. For example, the Institute of British Geographers set up a new study group in 1988, called 'Social and Cultural Geography'. In 2000, a new academic journal called *Social & Cultural Geography* was established, and it published a series of reports on 'social and cultural geography' in different countries. Over 20 country reports were published, primarily focusing on Europe and the Anglophone world,[15] further reinforcing the idea that there was little difference between the two.

For some social geography did not exist. For example, when Richard Peet wrote *Modern Geographical Thought* in 1998, he included a diagram that showed the development of schools of thought in human geography between 1850 and 2000 (Figure 0.1).

While cultural geography was represented as a key stream, social geography was not included at all. Instead, what we might think of as social geography is subsumed under offshoots from regional geography and environmental determinism: radical-Marxist geography, structuralism, and realism-structuration-locality. There's no sense, in the book, that social geography exists as a standalone area of the discipline. The erasure of social geography, at least in Peet's discussion, was complete.

> ## BOX 0.4 THE 'CULTURAL TURN'
>
> A renewed focus on questions of culture in Geography, influenced by the development of cultural studies in British universities (key people in cultural studies included Stuart Hall and Raymond Williams). This led to the development of a 'new cultural geography' from the 1980s onwards. New cultural geographers began to engage with many of the issues that had previously been the focus of social geography, including power and difference in the formation of cultures and lives.

Figure 0.1 shows that the definition and place of social geography in the discipline of Geography keeps changing. Now, in the twenty-first century, social geography is more prominent, and again diverging from cultural geography. New textbooks on social geography are being published – including this one. Calls have been made to 'reinvigorate' social geography, including by one of the authors of this book, Professor Kath Browne. The core issues that social geographers consider, such as inequality and injustice and marginalisation and power, are more pressing than ever, and their significance has been intensified with the effects of the global COVID-19 pandemic. And social geography has both returned to its roots, showing a concern for environmental issues and social justice, and also expanded its understanding of the social to include the 'more-than-human': the objects and infrastructures that influence the social and the spatial.[16] What we show in this book is that social geography is diverse and more appropriately named social geographies. We begin this by questioning the story we have just told of the official version of the history of social geography.

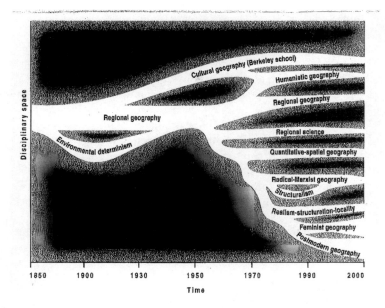

Figure 0.1 Richard Peet's Schools of Modern and Postmodern Human Geographical Thought.

Source: Peet, Richard. *Modern Geographical Thought*. (Malden MA and Oxford: Blackwell Publishing, 1998), p. 10.

III. DECOLONISING SOCIAL GEOGRAPHY: A DIFFERENT VIEW FROM THE MARGINS

You will have noticed that, in our overview, the history of social geography is partial and geographically specific. We write mostly about men, based in the English-speaking world or in Europe. We write about specific approaches, such as Marxism or the cultural turn, and pay less attention to other ways of thinking about or doing social geographies. The people and topics we chose to highlight give an insight into our training as social geographers, and our particular backgrounds: just one of us completed our PhD in the country where we were born, and three of us studied at universities in the US and the UK. We are now all living in countries that were former British colonies – India and Ireland – and that are still shaped by that experience of colonialism (Box 0.5 and Box 0.6). Writing in English is just one of the obvious ways in which our social geographies still have colonial traces.

Social geography, like the discipline of Geography more broadly, is marked by its colonial past. Geography is one of the academic disciplines that benefited from its positioning in relation to colonialism, particularly European colonialism. In countries like France and Germany and Britain, geographers made themselves indispensable to the process of colonialism. They used their skills in mapping and navigation, in identifying natural resources that could be exploited, and in interpreting the relationship between environment and people to provide useful knowledge to colonisers to pursue their aims and enhance their control. In a wide range of countries and cities, geographers set up geographical societies where they reported on their travels and explorations. This created a sense of excitement about geography, and it also led to the establishment of Geography as a recognised academic discipline in universities across Europe.

BOX 0.5 COLONIALISM

The process by which one country gains control over another country and exploits that relationship for its own benefit. Control can be political, economic, military, social, cultural, or a mixture of these. Many European countries were involved in colonialism as colonial powers: of these, Britain had the most extensive range of colonies.

BOX 0.6 TYPES OF COLONIALISM

There are two broad types of colonialism: settler and resource. Under settler colonialism, large numbers of people from the colonial power move to the colony and displace the original inhabitants. Ireland is an example of settler colonialism. Under resource colonialism, the emphasis is on extracting the colony's wealth. India is an example of resource colonialism. It's important to note that, under colonialism, wealth was also extracted from Ireland, and British people also settled in India.

INTRODUCTION 11

If we return to Richard Peet's diagram, we can see that an approach to geography known as 'environmental determinism' was important in this period of European colonialism. Environmental determinism is a significant part of the story of social geography: Peet suggests that it was the forerunner to a wide range of contemporary geographical approaches. One of the key impacts of environmental determinism was that it reinforced a hierarchical understanding of the world that continues today, because it claimed that certain environments, and consequently certain types of people, were more developed or civilised than others. Not surprisingly, environmental determinists tended to think that European environments and climates were more conducive to civilisation. In contrast, environments and climates in areas that were being actively colonised – such as Africa and Asia – were portrayed as backward and uncivilised and difficult. When Europeans moved to colonies, there were concerns for their moral wellbeing. These settlers were often diagnosed with a disease called tropical neurasthenia: common in colonial times, but no longer widely diagnosed. Tropical neurasthenia referred to the problems faced by white colonial settlers in the tropics: both physical and psychological. In particular, it referred to people behaving outside the restrictive norms of colonial society. The diagnosis of tropical neurasthenia further reinforced the idea that colonised peoples were less civilised due to their environment, since interacting with them and living where they lived gave rise to a 'deterioration' in the behaviour of colonial settlers.

> ## BOX 0.7 ENVIRONMENTAL DETERMINISM
>
> Environmental determinism is the belief that a person's character is *determined* by their environment, particularly the climate of the place where they were born and lived. This was used to justify particular hierarchies that saw some people/groups as better than/more civilised and so on when compared to others.

Some of the key figures in environmental determinism include Friedrich Ratzel, Ellen Churchill Semple, and Thomas Griffith Taylor (Box 0.7). We introduced Ratzel earlier, as one of the originators of social geography. Semple was from Kentucky in the US, and she went to Germany to study with Ratzel though, as a woman, she wasn't allowed to sit beside male students. When she returned to the US, she taught in several universities, and was the first female elected as president of the Association of American Geographers (AAG)[17] in 1921. Griffith Taylor was born in England but moved to Australia with his family as a teenager. He was also elected president of the AAG, in 1940, and worked in the US and Australia. These are just some of the proponents of environmental determinism, and they were leading international figures in the development of geography. This matters, because it has profoundly shaped how geographic knowledge about people and place has developed. As we will show you in this book, geography is still affected by colonial ways of thinking that see some people and some places as more important than others.

Around the time that Ratzel and Semple were advancing their theories of environmental determinism, people who were the subjects of colonial rule were fighting for independence and autonomy. Their efforts to resist colonial rule are collectively known as anticolonialism, and this led to former colonies becoming nominally independent, particularly in the period after World War II (Box 0.8). We say 'nominally', because most former colonies continued to be economically and socially dependent on their former colonial rulers. This has been described as neocolonialism, a process of indirect control replacing the direct political control that existed under colonialism.

BOX 0.8 ANTICOLONIALISM

Anticolonialism is a political movement dedicated to the abolition of colonial rule. There is a wide variety of anticolonial movements, including pacifist and direct action.

The persistence of neocolonialism has led to calls for decolonisation. Perhaps the most well known came from Kenyan writer Ngũgĩ wa Thiong'o. His book, *Decolonising the Mind*, was published in 1986. In it, he announced that he would no longer write in English, but instead would only write in Kiswahili and Gĩkũyũ. To explain his decision, he wrote that "The domination of a people's language by the languages of the colonising nations was crucial to the domination of the mental universe of the colonised".[18] To counter this, Ngũgĩ wanted to move away from English, in order to insist on the significance and importance of the Kenyan languages that had been devalued under colonialism. Decolonising the mind, then, meant challenging inherited colonial hierarchies about language, about people, and about place.

In the twenty-first century, there have been growing calls to decolonise geography. This is part of a broader movement to decolonise university curriculums and the construction of knowledge more generally. If we look to Ngũgĩ for guidance, this means that we pay attention to what colonialism has done to *what* and *how* we teach, research, and learn. The movement to decolonise geography has a long history. However, it came to prominence in 2017 when the Royal Geographical Society with the Institute of British Geographers decided that the theme of their annual conference would be 'Decolonising Geographical Knowledges: Opening Geography to the World'? In conjunction with this, a number of British geographers wrote widely read journal articles about the need to decolonialise geography, and have since continued to publish articles and books on this topic. Other British geographers raised concerns about the conference theme. They argued that it paid lip-service to decolonisation and failed to address broader structures, institutions, and practices that developed from, and continue to reinforce, colonial dominance.[19] In many ways, this criticism was reiterating a problem that geographers around the world have been expressing for many years. Canadian geographer Lawrence Berg wrote that geographies produced in the US and the UK – sometimes called Anglo-American geographies – are treated as 'unlimited' or global in their importance and reach; while geographies produced in other countries and contexts are seen as 'limited' or local or parochial.[20] The colonial practices that remain in the discipline of Geography are widespread. They include the ongoing division of places and people into often unacknowledged hierarchies. They include the prioritisation of knowledge from particular places and people, and the devaluing of knowledge from elsewhere. They include the persistence of racism and white supremacy in the discipline, and the marginalisation of the perspectives and experiences of Black and Indigenous geographers.

Calls to decolonise geography build on or are connected to a wide range of other efforts to challenge how geographic knowledge is produced, such as feminist geographies, Indigenous geographies, Queer geographies, Black geographies, and critical geographies. Feminist geographies draw attention to the ways in which women were written out of geographic scholarship and insist on the inclusion of women as researchers and as researched, at the same time advocating for alternative approaches to learning about people's experiences. Indigenous geographies highlight the ways in which colonialism erased or marginalised Indigenous people and drew attention to the alternative ways of understanding the world – particularly the relationship between people and their environment – provided by Indigenous knowledges. Queer geographies challenge how heterosexual and gendered norms are presumed in geographical studies (for example studying 'households' that are presumed to be heterosexual family units with a male 'head'). Black geographies insist on the importance of Black spatial agency. Critical geographies highlight the spatialities of power and insist on the importance of praxis in challenging socio-spatial inequalities (Box 0.9). All these different approaches to Geography and to the construction of geographic knowledge challenge dominant understandings, and seek to expand how Geography is understood, researched, taught, and practised. As such, they show that calls to decolonise Geography should not be presented as new, but instead build on the efforts of geographers across a wide range of times and places, many of whom were marginalised when they called for change.

BOX 0.9 PRAXIS

Praxis means *theory in practice*; or a practice that cannot be separated from theorising. Praxis seeks to destabilise the separation of theory (an idea or set of ideas about how the world, or aspects of it, work) and practice (concrete material actions). Often, the term praxis is used to refer to attempts to bring about change, which are deeply embedded in ideas about how the social world works and can be imagined differently.

INTRODUCTION 15

Drawing inspiration from broader calls to decolonise geography, we believe that it is very important to decolonise social geography, creating diverse social geographies that recognise how geographies are created matters to knowledge and therefore what happens in the world. Our approach to decolonising social geographies is organised around three important principles:

1 An emphasis on understanding social geographies from the 'margins' rather than from the 'centre'. We recognise the challenges with this, given our own complicated positionings, but in developing the book we have sought to prioritise the experiences and knowledge of people from outside the Anglo-American core.
2 Social geographies as praxis (that is theory and practice/thinking and doing together). Because of this, the book foregrounds activism and social change, and uses examples of praxis to show what social geography is and could be.
3 Seeing social geography as relational rather than hierarchical. This means thinking and doing in ways that do not see one person/group/identity/thing as better than another. One way in which we emphasise relational approaches to social geography is by highlighting key themes that are of relevance to people across a range of different contexts, thus showing connections rather than differences. Another way is in the final chapter, where we report on our conversations about social geography from our very different locations and perspectives.

If decolonising is about the *what* and the *how*, we attempt to address each of these by crafting a more inclusive, participatory, and relational approach to writing this textbook and to telling the past, present, and future stories of social geography.

IV. WHY GEOGRAPHY? TOOLS, CONCEPTS, SKILLS

Earlier, we defined social geographies as social lives that are made in space and place, and that in turn shape the spaces and places where they exist. In this section, we want to highlight the 'geographies' of social geography, and to briefly introduce and explain the themes that help us make sense of people's social lives across space and place.

We start with core concepts across the discipline of Geography: *space and place*. These concepts are often used interchangeably because they both refer to *where*, but they differ in some important ways. The term 'space' indicates a location that can be identified and fixed, for example using a grid reference. The implication is that space is objective. In contrast, the term 'place' refers to how people feel about or give meaning to specific locations, in other words subjective. When thinking about *where*, social geographers have tended to favour space over place, even though the distinctions between the two are often blurred. This may be because of how social geography developed, in particular the influence of urban studies and Marxism. Both urban studies and Marxism were more interested in space, in contrast to cultural geography and humanism which tended to emphasise place. However, social geographers have moved beyond an understanding of space as an objective location, using concepts such as 'social space' and 'spatiality' (Box 0.10 and Box 0.11). The two terms are used in a variety of ways, but their key contribution is to show the interrelatedness of space and the social: that means that social relations and interactions affect or influence space, and that space in turn affects or influences the social. In other words, space is not just an objective location, but it is actively created and/or changed by people, and at the same time makes social lives (Box 0.10).

BOX 0.10 SOCIAL SPACE

Perhaps the best-known use of the term is by the French urban theorist Henri Lefebvre, who famously said that "(Social) space is a (social) product"[21]. By this he means that space is always produced by people, rather than being something that exists apart from or separate to people. This is important for social geographers, because it shows the relationship between society, the social, and space.

BOX 0.11 SPATIALITY

For many social geographers, spatiality is a more useful concept than space. Spatiality is concerned with the relationship between space and society, which is an ongoing process: society, or people, change space; space, in turn, changes society; and this is repeated so that it isn't possible to have one without the other. Because of this, there is an infinite number of spatialities, at a range of different scales.

INTRODUCTION **17**

In this book, we use both space and place when we are talking about *where*. For us as geographers, the key point is that *where* matters when we consider how our lives are lived. *Where* – spaces and places – provides us with opportunities and/or imposes limits on our potential. In turn, we seek to preserve and/or change the spaces and places we inhabit, whether this is through practice or protest. Spaces and places are, as geographer Doreen Massey suggests, "always in the process of being made" and it is this process of making that is the focus of social geographies and this book.[22]

If space and place – the *where* of social life – are always in the process of being made, then *time – the when of social life* – is also important to consider. Like space, there can be a tendency to think of time as objective and fixed. Time is certainly measured and quantified: think of how we may be required to record our time spent at work, or how we pay for access to services by time (e.g. bicycle hire). However, our experiences of time suggest an alternative. Think of how quickly time passes when you are absorbed in an activity, like a class in social geographies! Or remember how slowly time passes when you are bored or tired at work, and just want to go home. As a child, time can seem infinite; as you age, time can appear to rush by.

Spaces and places change and are changed over time, which has led many social geographers to argue that space and time should always be considered in conjunction. Swedish geographer Torsten Hägerstrand drew attention to this when he developed the concept of 'time geography'. Hägerstrand developed this concept from his research on people's everyday lives in urban settings but extended it to consider broader spatial and temporal scales, for example international migration or the time geography of an entire lifetime. Time geography was popular in the 1970s but was later replaced by the concept of time-space (or, alternatively, space-time). Influential geographers such as David Harvey and Doreen Massey were to the forefront in insisting that space and time have to be considered together.

Of course, these accounts of place, space, and time are rooted in specific contexts. Peter Merriman describes them as Anglophone and Western and points out that different languages and different cultures have other ways of understanding time and space.[23] For example, the French word *espace* is thought of as open and free, in contrast to the German word *raum* which is located and constrained. Indigenous scholars highlight alternative approaches to understanding place and space and time. For example, Māori in Aotearoa New Zealand see place as inextricably linked to identity: the word 'whenua' is used to describe both land and placenta.[24] Bawaka Country, which is a place/space *and* a collection of Indigenous people and academic geographers, use the concept of *gurrutu* (Box 0.12) to provide alternative understandings of place/space that are relational and emergent and co-becoming. They describe it in this way:

> Everything has *gurrutu*. The land, the animals. A child says, 'Look at that rock.' We answer, 'Oh yes, that is your *märi*, your grandmother.' Another might say, 'Look at that whale.' We answer, 'That is your *yapa*, your sister.'[25]

BOX 0.12 *GURRUTU*

Gurrutu is a system of kinship that underpins the social lives and worlds of Yolŋu people in Australia. Yolŋu are Indigenous inhabitants of northeastern Arnhem Land in the Northern Territory of Australia. *Gurrutu* charts the complex relationships between people and all kinds of things – for example, flora, fauna, landscape, weather, stories – that together become a known place/space called Bawaka Country.

Concepts such as *queer time* and *crip time* offer alternatives to dominant understandings of time: they illustrate that, rather than one agreed upon and linear objective time that follows the social-psychological development of an individual, there are multiple temporalities (Box 0.13 and Box 0.14).

BOX 0.13 QUEER TIME

The concept of queer time offers an alternative to conventional understandings of the human life-course (e.g. progressing from birth and childhood in a heteronormative family through education to work to marriage to family). Conventional understandings are sometimes described as *chromonormativity*.

INTRODUCTION   19

> **BOX 0.14 CRIP TIME**
>
> Often placed in opposition to *clock time*, crip time is used to describe the different and unpredictable relationships that disabled people have with time. Crip time presents a counter to the straight and linear understanding of time.

We've introduced these different ways to consider place, space, and time because of our commitment to a decolonial approach. These alternative definitions are situated in the 'margins', they are relational rather than hierarchical, and they make different types of social geographies possible.

Environment is another important concept to consider within social geography. Our account of the development of social geography highlighted early work on environment, which often meant the physical environment or the natural world. What this meant for social geography was a focus on the relationship between humans and the environment. In environmental determinism, the environment – particularly climate – was seen as most important: the environment determined human behaviour and civility (Box 0.7). More recently, that relationship has been inverted, and now the emphasis is on how humans affect the environment. There is a particular emphasis on the negative impacts of humans, for example through environmental pollution or destruction, or through anthropogenic climate change (Box 0.15). There is a particular concern with the global impacts of human activities on the environment, evident across the discipline of Geography as a whole. Indigenous geographies highlight both the destructive effects of human activities and a range of hopeful alternatives.[26]

> **BOX 0.15 ANTHROPOGENIC CLIMATE CHANGE**
>
> This is changes to climate caused by human action, such as burning fossil fuels. The scale of anthropogenic climate change, combined with other changes to the natural environment caused by human action, have led some commentators to describe the current period as the *Anthropocene*.

Space, place, environment, time: these are fundamental concepts that underpin our understanding of social geography. You'll remember that we defined social geography as the social lives that are made in space and place, and that in turn affect space and place. We have shown how space and place, like environment, are ways of describing *where*, and we have suggested that *where* is a very important issue for social geographers to consider. We have also shown that *where* is also connected to *when*, and that it is important to consider time together with space/place/environment.

How geographers think about *where* draws our attention to other key concepts that consider how *where* is organised and experienced. We'll start with *scale*. Like space and place, the meaning of scale is often debated and difficult to pin down. Scale is a very important concept in cartography, as it indicates the relationship between the size of what is being mapped and the size of the map itself. Small-scale maps show large areas, for example 1:250,000, where 1 cm on the map represents 250,000 cm in real life. Large-scale maps show small areas and provide more detail about the features contained in the map, for example 1:1,250, where 1 cm on the map represents 1,250 cm. The scale helps us to understand what has not been included on the map.

Cartographic scale is just one type of scale that geographers think about and use. Another approach to scale is sometimes called 'geographic scale'. At first, this tended to look at the different levels of human activity, such as the neighbourhood, the city, the region, the nation-state, and the global. Different people and different groups or organisations of people have different reach and impact: this reach and impact represents the different scales of social life. The assumption was that these different scales were organised hierarchically, with the global or the nation-state having more significance and importance than the neighbourhood. Often, the existence of geographic scale was taken for granted. Over time, though, geographers began to question this. Marxist geographer Neil Smith concluded that scale was socially produced: in other words, scales were the outcome of social life, rather than a neutral and pre-existing site of social life. Smith saw capitalism as the key aspect of social life that produced scale, though over time he also acknowledged how other forms of social difference also produced scale (Box 0.16). His insights are very important, because they challenged the idea that scale is hierarchical (one is more important than the other), and instead showed that scales are relational (that they relate to each other and co-create each other).[27]

BOX 0.16 CAPITALISM

A system of socio-economic organisation that dominates in today's world. Profit is the driving force of capitalism, and profit is made by selling goods and services (known as commodities) for more than they cost to produce. A small number of people make profit under capitalism – they are known as the *bourgeoisie*, and they control the resources that are needed to make profit (land, labour, and money). However, under capitalism most people do not make profit. Instead, they survive by selling their labour for wages. This group is called the *proletariat*.

Movement is another important concept for thinking about how *where* is organised and experienced. Movement is a central part of social life. For the vast majority of people, every day involves movement: within the places where we live; to and from places where we study or work; to and from places where we obtain the things we need to sustain our social lives. The everyday movement of people was an important focus for time geographers. However, movement is not confined to people: a whole range of non-humans also move regularly. This includes other living things, such as animals; it includes components of our environment, such as water and air; and it also includes objects that are designed for movement and objects that move. For social geographers, the movement of people – known as migration – has been a particular focus. However, social geographers have also been concerned with the ways in which people move. This includes changing modes of transportation: for example the replacement of walking with cars; the replacement of ships with airplanes; and the return to more environmentally friendly forms of transport such as cycling. And social geographers have also paid attention to how things move, such as the growth in containerisation, and the impact this has on social lives in space and place. Scales of movement have altered with technological changes, giving rise to new descriptions of the relationship between time and space, such as time-space convergence (Box 0.17).

BOX 0.17 TIME-SPACE CONVERGENCE

The process by which distant places are brought closer together because of technological changes. An example is the travel time between two 'global' cities, London and New York. At the start of the twentieth century, it took around five days to sail from London to New York. At the start of the twenty-first century, the fastest flight between the two cities took around five hours.

The changing understandings of scale and movement lead us to the next important concept, which is *relations*. Traditionally, geographers have written about the relationships between places and people in a hierarchical way. Examples of this include the way the world was divided spatially into core and periphery, or developed and developing; or social divisions between people on the basis of gender, or race, or sexuality. In all these cases, some places and people were seen as better than others, whether this was framed in terms of development or civilisation or capacity. In environmental determinism, the social and spatial were combined to create these hierarchies; and this practice continued in other, less explicit ways, such as the association of certain, stigmatised parts of the city with certain racial or ethnic groups. On one level, we can see hierarchies of people or places as relational, where the relationship is of superiority and inferiority. However, throughout this book, when we use the term 'relational', we have a different understanding. We are drawing on newer approaches within geography, such as 'networks' or 'assemblages'. Both these terms indicate *how people, places, and things are related or interrelated* in a *non-hierarchical* way. This means that the different components of networks or assemblages are not assessed in a way that compares one to the other and sees some components as more important or significant than others (Box 0.18 and Box 0.19). Given the extent to which the discipline of geography developed by making these types of value-laden comparisons, an emphasis on non-hierarchical relations offers a new way of thinking about social geography.

INTRODUCTION **23**

> **BOX 0.18 NETWORKS**
>
> Networks connect people, things, and places. They can be social, spatial, or both. The term is used in a variety of ways within social geography, for example to look at transport or infrastructure, or to consider the spatialities of social networks. Often, social geographers look at networks in combination with actors (which can be people and things), in an approach called actor-network theory.

> **BOX 0.19 ASSEMBLAGE**
>
> An assemblage is a whole that is made up of different parts that may or may not be otherwise connected, and that may or may not have connections with other parts or other wholes. An assemblage can include humans, non-humans, objects, groupings, ideas, and emotions. Within social geography, social movements are sometimes described and explained as assemblages.

Taken together, these core concepts – *place, space, environment, time, scale, movement*, and *relations* – show us how and why a geographical approach is important for thinking about the social. Social lives are lived and experienced in and across place, time, and scale. If we are to better understand social lives, we need to understand where and how they are grounded, what that grounding means and does, and how we can challenge the injustices of specific forms of grounding. These experiences and practices are always relational, and those relationships take multiple forms and go in many different directions. Spaces and places influence social lives, and social lives in turn influence spaces and places: across different time periods and different scales. Space and place are at the core of our interest in how the social might be reimagined and changed in ways that make material differences.

V. WHAT IS THE 'SOCIAL' IN SOCIAL GEOGRAPHY?

We have spent time showing how we understand geography, and why geography is important. We want to move next to explaining

24 INTRODUCTION

our understanding of the social in social geography. There are many ways of considering the social, evident in academic disciplines such as sociology and other social sciences. Our account focuses in particular on how the social intersects with geography: what does the social mean in space and place? We answer this by introducing a small number of key concepts here, and we will develop these further in later chapters.

Our starting point is *power*. We believe that power is always exercised by people, acting alone, in groups, or through social institutions that are created and maintained by people over space and time. Because power, like the social, is made by people, it means that it is not inevitable, or 'just there'. Power can be exercised directly by those in positions of authority, such as governments or police forces or armies. Power can also be exercised indirectly by those in authority, by creating the conditions that lead people to behave in a particular way. This is sometimes called *hegemony* (Box 0.20). Of course, power is not unidirectional, and power can also be exercised by those with less authority or resources. This type of power is sometimes described as resistance or resisting power, but this description is limited, because it suggests that it is a reaction rather than being developed in its own right. A social movement concerned with bringing about social change could be described as resistance, but it is also seeking to create something new.

BOX 0.20 HEGEMONY

This concept was developed by the Italian writer and activist Antonio Gramsci. It refers to how a minority group exercises control over the majority by convincing them to act against their own best interests, that is, through a manufactured consensus.

Within social geography, power is used to understand inequalities, resistances, and difference. One way that power is thought of is through the ability to create and at times change space and place, and the ability for spaces and places to effect change in how social life is lived. For example: many governments are now building border walls to separate their territory from another territory. A well-known example is the border wall between the US and Mexico, but this is just one of a growing number of border walls being built around the world. When a border wall is built, a government exercises its power to show the extent of its territorial control, and in doing so it changes the space of the border. When a border wall is built, it also changes how the border is used and experienced, and it makes it much more difficult for some people to cross the border. Power can be exercised across a range of different scales, often simultaneously: from the government decision to build a border wall to the teams who build and maintain it to the individual border guard who decides whether or not the person standing in front of them will be permitted to cross from one territory to another.

Another way power operates is through self-surveillance and ensuring that we act in a way that is 'appropriate'. This comes from Michel Foucault's understanding of power and biopolitics (that is, the politics that affects our everyday lives in ways that are not only about directly imposing laws and sanctions but also about other ways of control). In this understanding of power, we make sure that we act within certain codes/norms that are considered 'normal' or 'common sense'. This can be anything from making sure you stop at a red light (in case you might get in accident or be 'caught' breaking the law), through to how same-sex and same-gender couples carefully regulate where they hold hands or show affection. No one has to tell you how to act, but if you act outside of acceptable codes and norms you may be verbally corrected (with the aim of shaming you into behaving 'appropriately'), physically abused or even risk extreme violence. Social geographers are particularly interested in the negative impacts of power on space, place and social lives, such as domination, marginalisation, oppression and precarity.

The next important concept is *identity*. As with other concepts, identity is used in many different ways. There are two important starting points: identity can be understood first as how we see ourselves, and second as how others see us. Sometimes those understandings overlap, but often they don't. This is the social or relational aspect of identity: it is defined both with and by others, but we may not like how others see and define us. Because of this, sometimes identity is defined with reference to the relationship between 'Self' and 'Other', where Self connotes the individual and Other indicates who is not like the Self.

26   INTRODUCTION

Aspects of identity that are often highlighted include gender, race, caste, ethnicity, sexuality, disability, religion, and nationality. Identities can lead to the formation of communities, or the development of solidarities, as people recognise their connections and similarities. However, identities can also result in the identification of difference, as groups seek to mark themselves as different and, in the process, to mark the identities of others as inferior and/or threatening. This is sometimes described as *Othering*. Othering leads to hierarchies: in recent years, this has included the denial of rights to women, Black people, Dalits,[28] queer and trans people, for example, because their identities are seen as less important, deviant, and/or as undermining the status quo.

As social geographers, we are particularly interested in two aspects of identity:

1   The first is *how identities are connected to space and place.* How are particular identities seen, as in or out of place, and what does this mean for social lives? As an example, the historic association of women with private spaces, such as the home, meant that women in public spaces – such as a city street at night – were seen as deviant and out of place. This gives rise to processes of inclusion and exclusion. The association of women with private spaces excluded them from full participation in public spaces (including by shaming women who were out in public so that women stayed in private), and women had to fight to be considered to belong in public. More recently, the relationship of identity to space and place has been described as 'belonging': of course, claiming belonging can also give rise to social and spatial exclusion (see Box 1.10 and Box 2.6). We really like how the Italian writer Claudio Magris describes the relationship between identity and space. He wrote that "Every identity is also a horror, because it owes its existence to tracing a border and rebuffing whatever is on the other side".[29]

2   The second aspect of identity that social geographers are interested in is *how identities are mobilised in space and place in order to bring about change.* One of the visible ways in which this happens is through protests, for example marches through the streets of cities. People form communities of solidarity to transform space and place, even if temporarily, in order to advocate for change. Social movements also organise around shared identities and solidarities to bring about

change in specific places, whether this is in local neighbourhoods, or in cities, across a country as a whole, or globally. In India, farmers organised collectively to oppose agricultural reforms that had been introduced by the Indian government; their social movement included mass protests in and around the Indian capital, New Delhi,[30] as well as local meetings, lobbying, and political pressure. When we consider identities in space and place, this does not just mean physical spaces and places. Virtual spaces and places – such as online communities and online activisms – are increasingly important when we think about the relationship between identity and space/place.

3   The third important issue for social geographers to consider is *how we can imagine and build better social lives in space and place*. This is future oriented, and concerned with how we might work together to change the world we live in for the better. One of the ways in which we do this is by identifying and challenging social and spatial hierarchies that can be formed through governments/authorities but also through commonsense norms. Another way is to consider how these hierarchies are used to diminish the quality and potential of social lives in place and space. Both these approaches challenge how power is used to marginalise or exclude. However, it's also important that we look at how communities and solidarities may emerge or be developed in place and space, whether physical or virtual, and seek to support those alliances and networks to reimagine our social lives to be more open, more inclusive, and more transformative. A reimagined social geography, as we advocate in this book, offers one important way to do this work.

VI. MAP OF THE BOOK

In this book, we introduce you to how social geography offers possibilities for imagining and building better social lives in space and place. Usually, books start with identifying the problems and then looking at the way people seek to address them. This book starts with the changes that are possible. In Chapter 1, we consider how people can act in solidarity to bring about change. We show how communities develop in and through place; and how these communities become involved in activism directed towards change. In Chapter 2, we focus on the geographies of difference, looking at how difference is made in and through place, and what this means for human and more-than-human lives. Chapter 3 is concerned with the geographies of precarity. We use the concept of a 'liveable life' to ask questions about whose lives matter, where and when; and to show the impacts of this on people who experience precarity. In Chapter 4, we discuss movement and mobility, showing the relationship between the movement of people and things and the places they move to and from. In the conclusion, we discuss the contested meanings of social geography and speculate on its possible futures. We do this through a conversation between the four of us where we draw on our different backgrounds and experiences and interests and our different hopes for change.

We deliberately start with the possibilities for change and then introduce the ways in which power creates difference and precarities and inequitable mobilities. This means that across the chapters there are conversations around geographies of power and around hope for change. We introduce and define key concepts to help you better understand and navigate these areas. These concepts, including those in this chapter, reemerge throughout the book. They are an important part of the connections and conversations that finish in the conclusion, and they are directly related to where we are located and coming from. The collective term 'we' is used throughout the book and this chapter. This is because the book is written collectively between four authors. The usage of 'we' can also mean a universalising tendency, where the views of the dominant group is meant to apply to all. As the authors of this book, we do not subscribe to this universalising 'we'. The substantive content and examples in this book are meant to hold the differences and diversities in the usage of the 'we'. 'We' created this book and who and where we are matter to the examples we used. In the conclusion and throughout the book, the differences and diversities between us are not erased but juxtaposed in a spirit of collective thinking and writing.

Because of who we are and where we reach, as well as the reach of social geographies, we both draw on a wide range of examples across places in the Global South and North to illustrate the broader relevance and significance of social geography; and acknowledge that our efforts are always limited. No one book could cover the entirety of the discipline or indeed the global contexts. Instead, we hope further work will come to do this and we seek to develop a social geography inspired by decolonial and anticolonial thinkers that contest how these kinds of geographies are often written. In your journey through the book, we hope you will be inspired to see how a social geography perspective helps you to see the connections and differences between people around the world, striving for better lives, and allows you to imagine and work to create those better lives in space and place.

In this chapter we have given you starting points not only to think about the upcoming chapters or the module or other academic pursuit you are reading this for, but also because we believe that thinking about the world using social geographies helps us to understand it in a way that makes meaningful change. We want you to use what you have learned here to think about your social life and to recognise that where it takes place matters to what happens. We want you to consider how power relations play a part and how they might be addressed in more equitable and just ways. As you read through this book, our hope is that you find more tools to do this, and we start with a chapter that shows that change and transformation is possible.

NOTES

1 Buttimer, A. (1968) "Social geography". In *International Encyclopedia of the Social Sciences*. The Macmillan Company and the Free Press. Available online at https://researchrepository.ucd.ie/bitstream/10197/10722/1/SocialGeography.pdf.

2 Rogers, A., N. Castree and R. Kitchin (2013) "Social geography". In *A Dictionary of Human Geography*. Oxford: Oxford University Press.

3 Del Casino, V. (2017) "Social geography". In D. Richardson, N. Castree, M. F. Goodchild, A. Kobayashi, W. Liu and R. A. Marston (eds.), *The International Encyclopedia of Geography*. John Wiley & Sons, Ltd. https://doi.org/10.1002/9781118786352.wbieg0874.

4 Ahmed, A. (1999) *Social Geography*. New Delhi: Rawat Books, p. 15. This built on Raza's earlier work: see Raza, M. (1979) *A Survey of Research in Geography 1969–72*. Bombay: Allied, pp. 63–64.

5 Pain, R., J. Gough, G. Mowl, M. Barke, R. MacFarlene and D. Fuller (2001) *Introducing Social Geographies*. London and New York: Routledge, p. 1.

6 Valentine, G. (2001) *Social Geographies: Space and Society*. Harlow: Prentice Hall, p. 1.

7 Panelli, R. (2004) *Social Geographies: From Difference to Action*. London: Sage, p. 1, p. 3.

30 INTRODUCTION

8 Del Casino, V. J. (2009) *Social Geography: A Critical Introduction*. Oxford: Wiley-Blackwell, p. 15.

9 Smith, S. J., R. Pain, S. A. Marst on and J. P. Jones III, eds. (2010) *The Sage Handbook of Social Geographies*. Los Angeles and London: Sage, p. 1.

10 Del Casino, V. J., M. E. Thomas, P. Cloke and R. Panelli, eds. (2011) *A Companion to Social Geography*. Oxford: Wiley-Blackwell.

11 Newcastle Social Geographies Collective (2021) *Social Geographies: An Introduction*. Lanham, MD: Rowman & Littlefield, pp. 4–5.

12 Dunbar, G. S. (1977) "Some early occurrences of the term 'social geography'". *Scottish Geographical Magazine* 93(1): 15–20. https://doi.org/10.1080/00369227708736353.

13 Smith, N. (2001) "Marxism and geography in the anglophone world". *Geografische Revue* 3(2). Available online at http://geographische-revue.de/gr2-01.htm.

14 Harvey, D. (2009) *Social Justice and the City* (revised ed.). Athens, GA: University of Georgia Press, p. 11, p. 151.

15 The regions and countries covered were in Europe (UK, Ireland, France, Germany, Italy, Czech Republic, Denmark, Finland, Portugal, Greece, Switzerland, Norway, Hungary), North America (US, Canada, Anglophone Caribbean), Australasia (Australia, Japan, China, Taiwan, New Zealand, Southeast Asia) and just one in Africa (South Africa).

16 Ho, E. L.-E. (2022) "Social geography II: Space and sociality". *Progress in Human Geography* 6(5): 1252–1260. https://doi.org/10.1177/03091325221103601.

17 On 1 January 2016, the AAG changed its name to the American Association of Geographers in order to reflect the growing international membership of the organisation.

18 Thiong'o, Ngũgĩ wa (1986) *Decolonising the Mind: The Politics of Language in African Literature*. Woodbridge, Suffolk: Boydell & Brewer Ltd, p. 16.

19 Esson, J., P. Noxolo, R. Baxter, P. Daley and M. Byron (2017) "The 2017 RGS-IBG chair's theme: Decolonising geographical knowledges, or reproducing coloniality?" *Area* 49(3): 384–388. https://doi.org/10.1111/area.12371.

20 Berg, L. D. (2004) "Scaling knowledge: Towards a critical geography of critical geographies". *Geoforum* 35(5): 553–558. https://doi.org/10.1016/j.geoforum.2004.01.005.

21 Lefebvre, H. (1991) *The Production of Space* (trans. Donald Nicholson-Smith). Malden, MA and Oxford: Blackwell, p. 26.

22 Massey, D. (2005) *For Space*. London, Thousand Oaks, CA and New Delhi: Sage, p. 9.

23 Merriman, P. (2011) "Human geography without time-space". *Transactions of the Institute of British Geographers* 37(1): 13–27.

24 Simmonds, N., T. Kukutai and J. Rykes (2016) "Here to stay: Reshaping the regions through mana Māori". In P. Spoonley (ed.), *Rebooting the Regions:*

Why Low or Zero Growth Needn't Mean the End of Prosperity (pp. 79–105). Wellington, New Zealand: Massey University Press, pp. 83–84.

25 Country, B., S. Wright, S. Suchet-Pearson et al. (2016) "Co-becoming Bawaka: Towards a relational understanding of place/space". *Progress in Human Geography* 40(4): 455–475, p. 463. https://doi.org/10.1177/0309132515589437.

26 Parsons, M. (2023) "Governing with care, reciprocity, and relationality: Recognising the connectivity of human and more-than-human wellbeing and the process of decolonisation". *Dialogues in Human Geography* 13(2): 288–292. https://doi.org/10.1177/20438206221144819.

27 Jones, J. P. III, H. Leitner, S. A. Marston and E. Sheppard (2017) "Neil Smith's Scale". *Antipode* 49(S1): 138–152.

28 A Dalit individual is a former untouchable person in the caste hierarchy in the South Asian region. Dalit means broken and oppressed. Popularized by anti-caste intellectuals such as Jyotirao Phule and Dr. B. R. Ambedkar, Dalit as a socio-political category articulates the right to live a dignified and violence free life and do away with the oppressive Brahmanical caste order.

29 Magris, C. (1999) *Microcosms* (trans. I. Halliday). London: The Harvill Press, p. 38.

30 The book uses Delhi and New Delhi at several places. New Delhi refers to the national capital of India and Delhi the larger Union territory within which New Delhi is located.

FURTHER READING

BOOKS

Ahmed, A. (1999) *Social Geography*. New Delhi: Rawat Books.

Ali, H. A. (2023) *Introduction to the Social Geography of India: Concepts, Problems, and Prospects*. Abingdon and New York: Routledge.

Berg, L. D., U. Best, M. Gilmartin and H. Gutzon Larsen (eds.) (2022) *Placing Critical Geography*. London and New York: Routledge.

Blunt, A. and J. Wills (2000) *Dissident Geographies: An Introduction to Radical Ideas and Practice*. Harlow: Longman.

Jones, E. and J. Eyles (1979) *An Introduction to Social Geography*. Oxford: Oxford University Press.

Livingstone, D. (1992) *The Geographical Tradition*. Malden, MA and Oxford: Blackwell.

Newcastle Social Geographies Collective (2021) *Social Geographies: An Introduction*. Lanham, MD: Rowman & Littlefield.

Raju, S., M. S. Kumar and S. Corbridge (eds.) (2006) *Colonial and Post-Colonial Geographies of India*. New Delhi: Sage.

Smith, S. J., R. Pain, S. A. Marston and J. P. Jones III (eds.) (2010) *The Sage Handbook of Social Geographies*. Los Angeles, CA and London: Sage.

JOURNALS

ACME: An International E-journal for Critical Geographies. Available online at https://acme-journal.org/index.php/acme

Social & Cultural Geography. Available online at www.tandfonline.com/journals/rscg20

Tijdschrift voor Economische en Sociale Geografie. Available online at https://onlinelibrary.wiley.com/journal/14679663

MAKING SOCIAL CHANGE POSSIBLE

Communities, activism, resistance, and solidarity

I. INTRODUCING THE POSSIBLE

In their minds
I, who smell faintly of meat
my house where bones hang
and my street where young men
wander without restraint
making loud music from coconut shells
strung with skin
are all at the extreme end of our town
But I keep assuring them
We stand at the forefront.

Sukirtharani[1]

Activism, Resistance, and Solidarity can take many forms. We often focus on visible acts, such as marches or protests, but it is important to recognise that other forms are also powerful and effective. To demonstrate this, we open the chapter with the words of Sukirtharani, a female Dalit poet, originally written in Tamil and translated by Lakshmi Holmström. The poem describes a rural landscape in India. It demonstrates how caste is built into the landscape, with Dalits segregated to the far end of the village. It also shows how Dalits are represented by other castes: the idea that they 'smell faintly of meat' associates Dalits with dirt and disease; while the practice of making

DOI: 10.4324/9781003266877-2

loud music and wandering without restraint can be seen as disorderly and uncivilised. But Sukirtharani challenges this. Her poem addresses those from other castes as well as her fellow Dalits, in an act of solidarity and resistance. "I keep assuring them/We stand at the forefront" is a call to the communities at the margins – in this case Dalits – to change this narrative and to claim their place. It is also an act of resistance to the stereotypes of dominant and affluent communities. The poem turns the language of violence and victimisation into the language of resilience and change, in the process building new solidarities. It both shows the need for actions, and it also creates the possibilities of new worlds and new lives through social movements.

BOX 1.1 SOCIAL MOVEMENTS

Social movements are groups of people organised around a common goal, often social and/or political. Examples of social movements include civil rights; feminism; LGBTQI+ rights; and environmentalism. Many social movements have specific local forms even though the issues they address may be of global concern. Social movements may have either reactive or proactive goals. Reactive means that the members of the social movement are seeking to prevent something from happening. This action is sometimes called resistance, and can take place at a range of scales, from the local to the global (Box 1.4). For example, local groups may organise acts of resistance to proposed neighbourhood changes, such as closing a library or a children's playground. Environmental groups may organise acts of resistance against the construction of oil or gas pipelines in particular places, but with international support. An example of this was the resistance to the construction of the Keystone XL pipeline between Alberta, Canada and Nebraska, US. In contrast, proactive goals seek to bring about something new that previously didn't exist. This might include creating public spaces for play for children at a local level, or advocating for new legislation at national level. The common goals of social movements could take either or both forms.

With raging global inequalities, environmental crises and amid rising authoritarian regimes, we are simultaneously witnessing challenges and working towards shared futures and more socially just worlds. Sometimes, more socially just worlds can be seen in improved standards of living, better legal rights and policy interventions, or the unseating of dangerous political regimes. At other times, social change is the slow brewing of solidarities and the rise of diverse and creative modes of resistance. The latter might not necessarily result in immediate solutions or indeed any change, but the process of seeking change can make lives more liveable through coming together to challenge injustices. Geography teaches us that however distributed these movements are across space and place and diverse scales, there are possibilities for interconnections and solidarities. In the era of global connectedness, ideas of change travel and ignite social relations, sometimes in unimaginable ways. This works through circulation and diffusion as well as sharing of information across social media. An example of this is the Arab Spring of early 2011 (Figure 1.1). A vegetable seller

Figure 1.1 Collage Depicting the Arab Spring – Clockwise from top left 2011 protests in Egypt, Tunisia, Yemen, and Syria.

Source: Wikimedia Commons. https://commons.wikimedia.org/wiki/File:Infobox_collage_for_MENA_protests.PNG Published On 12 April 2011. This file is licensed under the Creative Commons Attribution-Share Alike 3.0 Unported license (https://creativecommons.org/licenses/by-sa/3.0/deed.en).

named Mohamed Bouazizi died by setting himself on fire on 4 January 2011, setting off protests across different countries in the Middle East, from Egypt to Tunisia to Yemen to Bahrain. The protests were about costs of living and state authoritarianism. Social media played an important part in making solidarities across these different countries and people.

In this chapter, we explore how people have come together in communities (the Niyamgiri protests in India), to create activisms (Repeal in Ireland), resistance (Indian Farmers Protest), and solidarities (Black Lives Matter). In providing these examples of hope and (at least partial) success, we show what is possible when people seek to bring about new social worlds where they live, work, and survive.

II. COMMUNITY: NIYAMRAJA PROTESTS

The Niyamraja protests in the state of Orissa, in the east of India, show how communities can come together to challenge environmental injustices (Figure 1.2, Box 1.2). Orissa has one of the largest deposits of bauxite in the world, with around 13% of the world's deposits found in the south and west of the state, many in hill districts with poor agricultural land. Bauxite is a valuable mineral as it is the main raw material for alumina, which in turn is used to make aluminium. The hill districts with large bauxite deposits are also home to a considerable number of Adivasis[2] and tribal communities, who have distinct cultural practices and specific understandings of and relations with nature. Adivasis and tribal communities did not always live in the hill districts, but were pushed there over centuries of migratory streams in order to keep the fertile plains under the control of the dominant caste Hindu economy. However, recently the less fertile hill districts have become more valuable because of their mineral riches. As a result, they have received attention from transnational corporations and the neoliberal Indian state who want to exploit the mineral reserves. In response, community groups have repeatedly organised to prevent mining activities and to preserve livelihoods and ways of life in the region.

BOX 1.2 COMMUNITY

Community is used to name all kinds of connections. Communities can be associated with neighbourhood areas, but can also be used to name connections between people that can relate to place (like a local community) or linked to identities (like lesbian, gay, bisexual, and trans communities). Communities can be formed and maintained through shared experiences, shared practices, and/or shared beliefs. While communities were often traditionally organised around physical proximity, increasingly communities are organised digitally, with more extensive reach. Although communities can assume that people are the same, have similar goals, and get along, communities are often fractured and complex. The power relations that bring people together and create inclusions can also result in exclusions.

The first attempt to exploit mineral resources began in 1993 when the state government of Orissa facilitated the formation of the Utkal Aluminium International Limited company. The goal of the new company was to exploit bauxite reserves in the Kashipur subdivision of the Rayagada district. The predominantly tribal and Dalit communities and villages were not consulted about this decision which would have significant consequences for their lives and land. They blockaded roads and prevented the company's surveyors from mapping the mineral reserves of the mountains located in the Kalahandi and Rayagada districts of South West Orissa. Bhagwan Majhi, an activist from the Kondh tribal group in the district, wrote a protest song called '*Dongoro Charibo Nahi*' ('We shall not leave the Dongor' – Dongor is a mountain range) in the mid-1990s, highlighting the Indigenous communities' concerns about the impacts of mining on the mountains: their home, a life force, God, and constitutive of their sense of selves. As India charts its development trajectory, it is relying on resource-rich regions of the tribal belt for raw materials, and on transnational corporations to extract the minerals. In these situations, what happens to the Indigenous people? They are uprooted and displaced. Their relationship with their surroundings, their culture and place: their social, religious,

38 MAKING SOCIAL CHANGE POSSIBLE

economic life worlds, and geographies are all discredited. They are told they are 'primitive', and development is what they need. Jacinta Kerketta, a prolific Adivasi poet from Jharkhand, another tribal dominated region, expresses the displacement and development in these terms:

> Leaving behind their homes,
> Their soil, and bales of straw
> Fleeing the roof over their heads, they often ask:
> O, city!
> Are you ever wrenched by the very roots
> In the name of so-called progress?[3]

A decade later, Bhagwan Majhi's protest song was again of relevance, as tribal communities in adjoining regions were similarly targeted and asked to move out of their homes to facilitate mineral extraction. In Rayagada district, in the Niyamgiri hills, Dongrias and Kondh communities worship the mountain as *niyamraja*, a sacred god that nurtured both them and the mountain. They were told that the land doesn't belong to them anymore. Instead, Vedanta Corporation, a transnational company listed on the London Stock Exchange, was given the right to mine the rich bauxite reserves. The corporation had signed a memorandum of understanding with the Orissa state government in 1997, and started acquiring land in 2002. The sanctity of the Niyamgiri hills was targeted by the powerful government, but the tribals did not let go of their habitat. This time, their song was rewritten to say '*gaon chorab nahi, jangal chorab nahi*' ('we shall not leave the villages, we shall not leave these forests'). Their fight to retain their sacred mountain went all the way to the Supreme Court of India. There, the tribals appealed for justice under the *Forests Rights Act 2006*, as dwellers and legitimate rights holders of these lands. In the Court, the following question arose: is the sanctity of these hills for these Adivasis only the rock at the top of the mountain where the tribals worship this god, or is the whole mountain sacred? The tribal communities who fought to protect their sacred mountain had to take on both the powerful state and a wealthy transnational corporation. In doing so, they had a different sense of their sovereignty of the land to those they opposed. The communities felt that even if the state denied them the right over their *Niyamraja*, they would fight for this right till their last breath.

Figure 1.2 Clockwise from top left, displaced tribal railway sit-in during Lanjigarh protests, 2011; Foot march by Dongrias and Kondhs, 2013; Protests outside Vedanta corporation in Bhubaneswar, 2016; London protests in the annual general body meeting of MNC, 2016.

Source: Foil Vedanta (www.foilvedanta.org).

Vedanta Corporation, which was involved in this suit, has had similar contestations in other parts of the world. In Australia and Zambia, for example, local Indigenous communities and groups raised concerns about the company's practices and the level of degradation of the land where their projects are located. In a number of these sites, under local pressure, Vedanta projects have been suspended or licences and contracts revoked. Local activists in Orissa began protesting Vedanta immediately, and media reports were picked up by national and transnational non-governmental organisations (NGOs), such as Amnesty International, Survival International, and Action Aid[4] (Box 1.3). These NGOs organised protests and media campaigns that drew attention to the Niyamgiri hills, and that helped to develop transnational networks of solidarity to support the communities' struggles. Environmental activists across the world, especially those organised as *Foil Vedanta*, started participating at the annual shareholders' meeting of the *Vedanta Corporation*

40 MAKING SOCIAL CHANGE POSSIBLE

and drawing attention to the violence and erasure of Indigenous cultures. They drew links and connections and developed networks of resistance between Niyamgiri, Delhi and London.

> ## BOX 1.3 NON-GOVERNMENTAL ORGANISATIONS
>
> Non-governmental organisations (NGOs) are generally not-for-profit organisations that operate separately from governments. They are usually directed towards a particular social or political goal. NGOs can be organised at a variety of scales, from local groups to transnational organisations. While NGOs can have a wide variety of goals, many NGOs have concerns with social issues such as human rights, the environment, or development. Advocacy and awareness are often the key focus of the work of NGOs.

Initially, the Supreme Court of India disregarded opposition to the Niyamgiri project on ecological grounds. However, in 2013 it decided that village councils should have the power to decide by referendum whether or not bauxite mining would be allowed on the Niyamgiri hills. In the months after the Supreme Court ruling, the 12 village councils all voted against allowing mining. These are smaller victories but raise larger questions about people and the relationship they have to places, and communities that lie at the fringes of state's recognition. The marginal status of these communities (for example, Adivasis not considered the so-called mainstream of Indian society) is reflected in how little their point of view is considered when their homelands are targeted for the 'benefit' of wider society. It is as if these Indigenous communities are not part of this society but are separate from it.

Though the Niyamgiri protests were rooted in local communities, they became global. When the scale expanded to include New Delhi and London, Australia and Zambia, it brought the protest from an invisible corner of India to centres of national and global power. In this way, it made agitation by a marginalised community visible nationally and internationally, and made it impossible for those in power to deny their existence. The Niyamgiri protests expanded the idea of community through the networks of solidarity that reached beyond the local. Had protests not reached the global scale, the stories could have been buried or co-opted, like many others that states or corporations exploit for growth.

One can find similar exploitative practices of the nexus of state and neoliberal capitalism and the resistance of Indigenous communities in other parts of the world, such as by Wangan and Jagalingou protestors in Queensland, Australia. The Queensland government decided to extinguish native title over 1385 hectares of land by giving it away to Adani Group for coal mining in 2019. This would result in Indigenous communities being forcibly vacated from their traditional lands which includes land used for ceremonial purposes. Wangan and Jagalingou communities resist this. Dalits, Adivasis, tribal, and Indigenous communities continue to resist the appropriation of their lives and lands in the name of growth across the world. Their resistance often takes varied shapes and forms, from localised challenges to global solidarity networks in the era of social media revolution.

III. ACTIVISM: REPEAL IN IRELAND

Changes to oppressive social orders can happen because people and communities act in solidarity towards common goals and shared visions of different lives, politics, and worlds. This work can be described as activism, and it is often resistant to the dominant ways things work to disadvantage and exclude people (Box 1.5). We use the Irish example of Repeal to show how activisms operate across national, local, and embodied scales.

BOX 1.5 ACTIVISM

Activism is trying to change the world. It is proactive with a goal such as political or social change. Geographies are important for activism, which is located somewhere and is often challenging geographically specific injustices. Activism can operate at various scales, from the transnational (like activism at the UN), national (protesting government policies or inaction around climate change for example), or regionally/locally (for example protesting abortion bans in various states/areas in the US). Activism is often seen as challenging or resisting dominant powers like the state, commercial companies, and organisations. However, activists can hold a wide range of political beliefs and positions, and are more accurately understood as people working to challenge social, political, or environmental orders and power relations. When people with political, economic, or social power use the term activist, it is often pejorative.

Repeal activism was directed towards the provision of abortion in Ireland. The name referred to the focus on repealing an amendment to the Irish constitution that had been made in 1983. This amendment – known as the 8th amendment or simply the 8th – effectively banned abortion in Ireland by adding a clause to the constitution asserting that "the state acknowledges the right to life of the unborn with due regard to the equal right to life of the mother". It was, in part, a reaction against the liberalisation of abortion rights in other countries, particularly the 1973 Roe v Wade Supreme Court decision in the US that provided a constitutional right to abortion.[5] However, it also needs to be understood in the specific context of Ireland, where the Catholic Church had a significant influence on government and public life. That influence was evident in the position and treatment of women and sexuality. For example, the constitution also prioritises women's work in the home, a position that resulted in the so-called 'marriage bar' that forced women to leave jobs on the public sector on marriage.[6] Pregnancy outside marriage was stigmatised, and there was only limited access to contraception.

The 8th amendment banned abortion in Ireland, but it could not stop women having abortions. Instead, it created a specific geography of abortion which was visible through the 'abortion trail' to England, where abortion was accessible to Irish residents, at a cost. The 8th also limited various forms of healthcare to those who were pregnant in Ireland, resulting in death or serious illness for many who were pregnant as doctors could not treat them if the 'life of the unborn' was at risk. Women of childbearing age also were subject to various pregnancy tests and checks before certain healthcare would be provided. Where they were found to be pregnant, certain forms of treatment, including cancer treatment, could be paused or stopped. Thus the geographies of abortion in Ireland related to *how* pregnant bodies were treated in hospitals, doctors' surgeries, and other health settings, and to *where* they accessed care. They also extended beyond healthcare settings into media, schools, workplaces, and other mundane spaces where shame, fear, and silence marked discussions of sex, abortion, and pregnancy.

Highlighting this issue and campaigning for change was a core feature of Irish feminist activism throughout the late twentieth and early twenty-first centuries, particularly as the effects of the 8th amendment – such as attempted bans on people travelling to England to access abortion – became clearer. A particularly troubling event happened in 2012, when Savita Halappanavar died of sepsis after being denied an abortion during a miscarriage; when she was refused a termination, she was told that Ireland was a 'Catholic country'. Her death heightened the attention on the issue of the 8th amendment and what it meant for healthcare in Ireland. There was widespread outrage and increased activism in response. This included a growth in local activist groups under the auspices of *ARC* (*Abortion Rights Campaign*), invigorated rallies and marches, increased political pressure, and a range of performance art protests to draw public attention to the issue. For example, one protest featured women walking with suitcases as a reminder of the abortion trail that thousands of Irish women were forced to undertake: this took place in both Dublin and London. Repeal jumpers (black with white Repeal across the front sold in aid of the Abortion Rights Campaign) became an iconic symbol of the movement to demand a new referendum. Renewed pressure and activism led to the Irish government announcing that a referendum on whether, or not, the 8th amendment should be repealed would take place in May 2018.

Years of activism – often small scale, often feeling ineffective – had led to this point. If the 8th was to be repealed, the levels of activism needed to be considerably increased. Throughout the decades the activisms that sought to Repeal the 8th amendment were fractured and groups did not always work together or necessarily agree with each other. Yet there was still the common goal of enabling full access to healthcare and access to abortion for those who are pregnant in Ireland. This common goal led to the creation of the umbrella 'Together for Yes' campaign, and various groups worked together under this banner. The national campaign organisation coordinated posters, messaging, and supported local groups and organisations that knocked on doors across Ireland to discuss the referendum and to seek to persuade people to vote Yes. These local organisations worked to include a broad range of people in door knocking, many of whom had never engaged in activism (Figure 1.3). The campaigning was undertaken in groups with those who were more experienced guiding and supporting those who were had not engaged before. Solidarities were created through this process of working together and the positive and negative reactions received at the doors. This local embodied form of activism deployed a tactic used in formal political processes in Ireland during election campaigns. In this context, knocking on doors to campaign for Repeal was a key activist strategy, bringing people together as activists who wouldn't see themselves as such.

Figure 1.3 Repeal Campaigners in Dublin North-West, 2018.
Source: Dublin North West Together for Yes.

Local campaigning was augmented by personal stories that became more public and prominent during the campaign for the referendum. A blog called 'In her shoes' posted harrowing stories of abortion, healthcare access and lives that were destroyed by the 8th amendment. These painful personal stories created a form of activism through being shared, helping to developing understanding, empathy and solidarities. Stories also featured in public televised and radio debates for those who sought a Yes vote. These debates were heavily regulated in mainstream media with exactly the same time afforded to the Yes and the No side. On social media there were attempts to stop those from outside of Ireland campaigning (there are limits on external funding sources that can be spent on referenda campaigns to avoid undue influence). Moreover, the social media tool 'Repeal blocker' was used by many to prevent No campaigners and commentators being seen on their Twitter timelines. Social media was also used to draw attention to public events such as the mural in central Dublin by well-known street artist Maser, featuring a red heart painted on a blue background that contained the words 'Repeal the 8th'. The mural was removed twice due to various legal and planning objections, specifically revolving around the demand for charities to be 'neutral'. The second removal of this art from the walls of an art gallery was made into a public activist event that drew more attention to the campaign and its goals.

Following the campaign, 66.4% of voters agreed that the 8th amendment should be removed from the constitution of Ireland. The win was formally announced and celebrated in Dublin Castle, a symbolically important site of Irish power. In addition, in the days following, a temporary memorial to Savita Halappanavar appeared in Dublin, remembering the woman who had lost her life as a consequence of the 8th Amendment (Figure 1.4). Final polls undertaken during the campaign suggested that decisions regarding voting intentions had been made some years before 2018. This indicates the importance of long-standing activisms by feminist communities over the decades in addition to the specific referendum campaign for a Yes vote that ran for just two months, from March 2018 to the vote in May 2018. The power of decades of Irish feminist activism can be seen in this outcome which changed access to healthcare for pregnant people. Though the 8th amendment was repealed, it's important to acknowledge that some activists raised concerns with how the national campaign was conducted. For example, there was an emphasis on those who needed abortions because of medical issues with babies and who could travel because of their Irish citizenship. These personal stories were seen as acceptable and recognised, while the stories of others – for example migrant women who did not have the right to travel to England – received less attention. Sex was still shamed as creating 'unacceptable' abortions.

The feminist activism that sought to enable abortion access and appropriate healthcare in Ireland is an example of creating legislative change through working together across multiple decades towards a common goal. It is built on challenging inequitable geographies of healthcare and access, and geographies are key to understanding how the activism used space to challenge injustice and create new legal landscapes. However, this change was imperfect and reiterated forms of power that continue to invisibilise and marginalise those who did not fit particular narratives of Irishness and Ireland. This is also geography – and part of the geographical imaginary of Ireland.

Figure 1.4 Temporary Memorial to Savita Halappanavar in Dublin, May 2018. Photo: Aoife Fox

IV. RESISTANCE: INDIAN FARMERS' PROTESTS

The Indian Farmers' Protests, which began in 2020, provide an excellent example of resistance (Box 1.6). These acts of resistance need to be understood within the broader structure of agriculture and farming in India. In the two decades after India gained independence from Britain (1947) food shortages and food crises were common. In part, this was connected to rapid population growth (1951, 360 million; 1971 570 million).[7] This was also connected to how rural societies were organised, in particular the small average farm sizes in India. To address food shortages in the 1960s/1970s, the government implemented a sweeping programme of increasing the yield of food crops – specifically rice and wheat. This was called the 'Green Revolution': it improved food security and resulted in India becoming a net exporter of some food grains. In the Green Revolution, more food was produced through modern agricultural methods, but the increased cost of inputs – seeds, fertiliser, machinery – meant that many small farmers incurred considerable debts that they struggled to repay. This transformed the social geographies of the regions where it was implemented, widening the gap in income, social status, and political power between the landed cultivators and the landless labourers. Some regions thrived, for example Punjab and Haryana, in the north west of India, where land holdings were relatively larger. In many other states, the Green Revolution increased dependence on financial capital, leading to indebtedness and, in turn, a growing toll of farmer suicides. The Green Revolution also changed crop patterns, pushed out traditional modes of farming, created water-intensive production modes, and engendered new forms of disparities. Dominant, landed castes were able to consolidate their power, launch political parties, and consolidate their gains. In some states, state procurement of crops became the norm. This worked through a system of minimum support prices: the minimum cost at which the government would buy certain kinds of grain from the farmer, regardless of the market price. This created a safety net for certain kinds of farmers, who also grew in power, thereby using their political clout to safeguard their economic interests. However, other farmers – many of whom were also Dalits – experienced bankruptcy, especially in the Vidarbha region in Maharashtra, western India. According to the National Crime Records Bureau 2019, around 10,281 persons belonging to the farming sector died by suicide in India, accounting for 7.4% of the total suicides in the year 2019.

BOX 1.6 RESISTANCE

Resistance in social geography refers to challenges to dominant, hegemonic social orders, or structures. Resistance is oppositional: it opposes something, usually a dominant power. Creating resistances is a form of empowerment. Resistances can be large scale, for example where environmental organisations stage large-scale resistances to oil companies. They can also be at the scale of everyday life. Small acts of resistance could occur, for example, when people are being exploited for work. Activisms can be seen as a form of resistance and can develop into social movements.

MAKING SOCIAL CHANGE POSSIBLE

In the summer of 2020, the government of India passed three controversial laws on agriculture: the *Farmers' Produce Trade and Commerce (Promotion and Facilitation) Bill, 2020*; the *Farmers (Empowerment and Protection) Agreement on Price Assurance and Farm Services Act, 2020*; and the *Essential Commodities (Amendment) Act, 2020*. The names of these laws suggest that they will have a positive effect on farmers: they include terms like 'empowerment' and 'protection' and 'promotion' and 'facilitation'. However, the main impetus for these laws was to create an open market for farm trade and to facilitate the entry of private capital and large corporations into the agriculture sector. The three laws were passed quickly with limited debate and threatened the edifice of the farming system. Farmers across all social classes feared that the laws would pose a threat to their livelihood and existence. Farming communities came together to resist these laws (Box 1.6), in the process creating a social movement.

Protests against these laws began in the state of Punjab, and then spread to Haryana and western Uttar Pradesh (Box 1.7; Figure 1.5). They were organised by local farmers' unions. After a couple of weeks of protests in Punjab, the local unions decided that agitating in their *pinds* (villages) was not enough and the protest had to move near the centre of power – the national capital, New Delhi (Figure 1.6). Farmers from Punjab, Haryana, and Uttar Pradesh all began to travel to Delhi to protest: some on foot, some in convoys of tractors. They were subsequently joined by farmers from more states, for example Assam, Goa, Kerala, Manipur, Rajasthan, Tripura, Telangana, and West Bengal. The protestors did not have an easy journey. They were stopped at multiple places. Some were beaten up and attacked with water cannons. However, they persevered, and reached the outskirts of Delhi in late 2020. Instead of returning to their villages, they camped on the outskirts of the national capital for 14 months, seeking to draw attention to their plight and the likely impacts of the three laws on their lives and livelihoods.

This mode of protest – of using tractors, trailers, and vans to create semi-permanent structures where protestors could stay for months – showed that the periphery was no longer content to be invisibilised by those at the centre and was instead looking to renegotiate these structures and boundaries. People from the rural periphery had now suddenly surrounded the national capital and created a virtual battlefield showcasing their collective community strength and solidarity in the face of governmental power. The protest itself created interesting new spatial pathways. Groups of men would set out every morning from their villages in Punjab and Haryana, travel to the protest site with necessary supplies, and then go back, thereby developing a kind of supply chain that connected this peri-urban space with the rural heartland. Squatting by itself was not a winning strategy but was sustained by the construction of these social and economic linkages, with some people permanently in the camps outside Delhi and others moving out and coming back. This allowed both the protest and the work of crop cultivation to be maintained throughout.

BOX 1.7 PROTESTS

The act of protesting can take numerous forms, but protests are always spatial. They are about taking up space on a temporary or a longer-term basis, often through disrupting everyday activities (for example through blocking streets). Protests are forms of resistance. They may contest specific forms of power that are seen as dominant, such as state power. Protests can also seek to stop something happening, for example environmental protests that seek to stop road or other developments. Protests do not have to be socially progressive and protests can seek, for example, restrictions on abortion.

During the 14 months of the protest, new social, spatial, and political relations were built because virtually whole villages were settled on the highways. This was extraordinary because, in the camps, a landless labourer from a Dalit community could be sitting next to, eating beside, or shouting slogans with a rich landed farmer. This reality is unthinkable in their native villages, where the schism between landowners and the landless is wide. In addition to the mixing of different castes, the camps also created new gender relations. Many women made their own *tolis* (small groups) and came to the protest by themselves, or as part of a village. For some, it was the first time they had crossed the boundary of their own

50 MAKING SOCIAL CHANGE POSSIBLE

Figure 1.5 Farmers' Union Protest against the farm laws in India 2020.

Source: Jaskiran (JK Photography), Wikimedia Commons. https://commons.wikimedia.org/wiki/File:Indian_Farmers%27_Protest_by_JK_Photography_14.jpg

This file is licensed under the Creative Commons Attribution-Share Alike 4.0 International license (https://creativecommons.org/licenses/by-sa/4.0/deed.en).

home or village. A 55-year-old farmer named Kandela from Haryana who had never protested previously described her experience in powerful words: "I didn't know what I was capable of beyond the expectations of me as a woman, a wife and mother, but I am here now, and I cannot be oppressed. I cannot be intimidated. I cannot be bought".[8]

The squatting was augmented by other strategies that expanded the geographical reach of the movement beyond the immediate blockade of New Delhi. Protestors used social media and digital tools, including diaspora WhatsApp groups, to raise awareness about their protest and to garner wider support, including financial resources to help sustain the camps. When international celebrities such as Rihanna backed the protest, the Indian government responded angrily. This shows that with digital reach, new geographies come into play: the possibility of a tarnished image on the international stage becomes a paramount concern for national politicians.

Figure 1.6 Farmers' Protest at Delhi's Tikri Border, 2020.

Source: Randeep Maddoke, Wikimedia Commons. https://commons.wikimedia.org/wiki/File:Farmers%27_Protest_at_Tikri_Border_-_29.jpg

This file is licensed under the Creative Commons Attribution-Share Alike 4.0 International license (https://creativecommons.org/licenses/by-sa/4.0/deed.en)

Things came to a head on 26 January 2021, when protesting farmers decided to hold their own parade of tractors in competition with the official national republic day parade, which includes marches by the three branches of the military, a show of state tableaux and military weapons. Eventually, the parade got out of hand, resulting in clashes with the police. On a day when the nation-state showcases its might on the national and global stage, the farmers chose to use their means of livelihood to march on the capital, and thereby lay claim to the republic.

The farmers' extensive efforts and ongoing protests were successful. The government rescinded the laws in October 2021, possibly in preparation for elections in Uttar Pradesh in early 2022. These successes challenged power relations and reworked the state, creating new possibilities. Thus, it is possible both to draw inspiration from how the farmers' protests used place – their villages, the camps, and the parade route – to advocate for change and at the same time see how the camps, in particular, changed place, by creating connections between people who are often segregated and separated. However, as with all social movements and resistances, the protests and the outcome also raise important questions about which communities can come this close to the centre of power? What kinds of protest geographies hold the most traction with the government? Which voices are heard by the government, and whose claims are deemed worthy of deliberation? At a time when members of Dalit, Bahujan, Adivasi, and Muslim communities in India are facing imprisonment for their participation in protests, questions remain about how place is made for some communities and some activists, but not others. These queries alongside the successes ask for us both to celebrate and to continue to critically engage with how more spatially equitable worlds can be created.

V. SOLIDARITIES: BLACK LIVES MATTER

The emergence of local, national, and global solidarities is evident in the Black Lives Matter movement, which emerged following the February 2012 killing of Trayvon Martin, a 17-year-old African American from Florida, by George Zimmerman. Zimmerman claimed that he shot Martin in self-defence, and he was acquitted of murder and manslaughter charges by a Florida jury in July 2013. Three Black women – Alicia Garza, Patrisse Cullors, and Opal Tometi – used social media to respond to the killing and acquittal, and to decades of unfair, exploitative, and violent treatment of Black people. They started a hashtag, #BlackLivesMatter (#BLM), which grew into a movement that they founded, also called Black Lives Matter (Figure 1.7). Supporters held protests across the US, often in response to the killings of Black people by police. Among the people whose deaths gave rise to protests were Eric Garner, killed in New York in 2014; Michael Brown, killed in Ferguson, Missouri in 2014; Freddie Gray, killed in Baltimore, Maryland in 2015; Philando Castille, killed in Minnesota in 2016; and Breonna Taylor, killed in Louisville, Kentucky in 2020. #BLM was one of several social movements that formed in response to the treatment and experiences of Black people and people of colour in the US. Others included Ferguson Action, Black Youth Project 100, Dream Defenders, Hands Up United, and Million Hoodies. #BLM became "the largest and most visible group",[9] and a member of the Movement for Black

MAKING SOCIAL CHANGE POSSIBLE   **53**

Lives (M4BL), a coalition of over 50 organisations with the overarching goal of Black liberation.[10] This movement moved into a global network of protest and solidarity that was co-constituted through online, media and in place events (Box 1.8).

BOX 1.8 ONLINE PROTESTS

Online protests can take various forms. Initially online petitions and protests were derided as 'armchair activisms' or 'keyboard warriors'. This was intended to indicate the futility of the protests and a lack of engagement with the issue. People were seen as lazy and not 'really' interested or willing to do enough to work towards change. However, it has become clear that 'hashtag protests' on social media can be hugely effective if they can gain significant support and momentum. They can attract support, influence thinking on an issue, and drive mainstream media stories and governmental change. In this way social media has become a space of activism and protest.

The distinction between online/offline protests has also been brought into question through the use of websites and social media to gather and arrange protests and offline events. These are then posted on social media gathering further support and creating communities and solidarities for those who were there, as well as those who did not attend. Such networks link the local spaces to the national and transnational, in the process developing communities and solidarities.

Linked to this, in August 2016 Colin Kaepernick – a professional football player with the San Francisco 49ers – first refused to stand for the national anthem of the US because of the treatment of Black people. Later, Kaepernick changed to kneeling for the national anthem, and he was joined by some of his teammates, like Eric Reid, and by a very small number of other NFL players during the 2016 season. Kaepernick was released from his contract, and it looked like the protests were waning, until Donald Trump became involved. During a rally in September 2017, Trump commented that he'd love to see an NFL owner say: "Get that son of a bitch off the field right now. Out! He's fired. He's fired!"[11] He was referring

Figure 1.7 BLM Graffitied Wall in Harlem NY, US.

Source: Jules Antonio, Wikimedia Commons. https://commons.wikimedia.org/wiki/File:Black_Lives_Matter_graffiti_wall,_Harlem.jpg

This file is licensed under the Creative Commons Attribution-Share Alike 2.0 Generic license (https://creativecommons.org/licenses/by-sa/2.0/deed.en).

to Kaepernick and player protests, using language from his popular reality TV show, *The Apprentice*. In response, many more players took the knee, commenting that they wanted to show solidarity.[12] Slowly, taking the knee spread nationally, internationally, and to other sports, in shows of solidarity across a range of different scales (Box 1.9).

BOX 1.9 SOLIDARITY

Solidarity can occur between individuals, within a community or social movement, or between different organisations. An example is a strike, when a collective of workers (usually members of a trade union) withhold their labour and stage a picket outside their place of employment. Members of other unions may refuse to cross the picket line as an expression of solidarity. Combahee River Collective, a group of Black feminist lesbian women writing in the late 1970s, showed us how political movements attempt to fracture us while planning and executing social justice activisms. Instead, they argued for the importance of solidarities across different social groups.

Solidarity is a form of mutual aid. The anarchist geographer Pyotr Kropotkin thought that all social organisations – which includes both communities and social movements – were an extension of mutual aid, which he understood as people working to support each other. In Ireland, an example is the *meitheal*, where people come together in a local area to help with tasks such as agricultural harvest or developing shared neighbourhood facilities or helping to rebuild a damaged house.

#BLM protests gathered new momentum following the killing of George Floyd in Minneapolis, in May 2020. Floyd was murdered by a police officer, Derek Chauvin, who pinned him to the ground and kept his knee on his neck for over eight minutes.[13] The murder was filmed by bystanders and posted on social media, and quickly spread globally. This led to mass organising in the US, where over 500 Black Lives Matters events, involving over half a million people, were held on 6 June 2020. In addition to the US, there were #BLM protests in the UK, Canada, New Zealand, Australia, France, Germany, Poland, Sweden, Italy, Spain, Portugal, Ireland, Brazil, Mexico, Colombia, Japan, South Korea, Kenya, and Senegal, to name just a few. In Italy alone, for example, over 150 protest and solidarity events took place in the summer of 2020, many organised by pre-existing student, local, or migrant groups.[14] The 2020 protests took place against the backdrop of COVID-19 lockdowns, and social media was very important as a way to spread information about protests and to create connections and develop networks between local and other organisers.

One of the forms of #BLM protests was directed at public statues and monuments commemorating those who had been involved in the historic suppression of Black people. In the city of Richmond, Virginia, for example, protestors defaced a number of statues of Confederate generals on a street called Monument Avenue. Richmond, Virginia had been the capital of the Confederate States of America, and the statues were erected from 1890 onwards to commemorate leaders of the Confederate 'Lost Cause'. There had already been controversy about Monument Avenue in 1995, when a statue of Arthur Ashe was erected there. Ashe was a Richmond native: an African American who was born and grew up in the segregated city, and who became an internationally successful tennis player and social justice activist. Many people – both white and Black – opposed having a monument to a Black man on Monument Avenue, which at that point was only commemorating white men.[15] In May 2020, the statues that were defaced included those commemorating Robert E. Lee, Stonewall Jackson, and Jefferson Davis. In June 2020, the statue of Robert E Lee was toppled by protestors and, in that month, the Governor of Virginia ordered the removal of all statues commemorating Confederate generals from Monument Avenue. By September 2021, the only statue remaining on Monument Avenue was that of Arthur Ashe.

Across the Atlantic Ocean, protestors in the city of Bristol in England toppled a statue of Edward Colston in June 2020. Colston was born in Bristol in the seventeenth century. He became very wealthy because of his role as a slave trader: he joined the Royal African Company (RAC), which had a monopoly on the West African slave trade, in 1680. It is estimated that the RAC sold around 100,000 slaves in the Caribbean and the Americas between 1672 and 1689. Colston used some of his significant wealth for philanthropic causes in Bristol, such as schools and hospitals, and the statue was erected in 1895 to commemorate his donations, but without mentioning his role as a slave trader. For many years, campaigners in Bristol had been advocating for the removal of the Colston statue because of his connection to slavery. This finally happened in June 2020 through direct action, following the example of the US. The statue of Colston was pulled down, and protestors knelt on its neck for over 8 minutes, in a tribute to George Floyd. The statue was then dragged through the streets of Bristol and thrown into the harbour. The Mayor of Bristol, Marvin Rees, commented on the "historical poetry" of this, as he mentioned the punishments that slaves would have received at the hands of slave traders like Colston.[16]

The action of taking a knee and the slogan Black Lives Matter have since been repurposed for other contexts. People in different social and spatial contexts have taken a knee to protest against racism and to show solidarity with those who experience racism. For example, many soccer players regularly take the knee when playing for their national or club side. In the European men's soccer championships in 2020, the national teams of England, Scotland, Wales, Belgium, Portugal, and Switzerland all took the knee before some or all of their games. Some individual athletes and teams also did this during the 2020 Tokyo Olympics, as did cricket players in the T20 Men's World Cup. As for the slogan, in India the hashtag #DalitLivesMatter was used to draw attention to the continuing violence against Dalit or 'untouchable' persons across India. This drew from earlier digital organising called #DalitWomenFight, from 2014, which showcased the systemic violence against Dalit women through a self-respect march in India and US (Figure 1.8). In this way, #DalitLivesMatter built connections and solidarities with other movements such as #SayHerName and #BlackLivesMatter. In Ireland and Britain, the hashtag #TravellersLivesMatter highlighted the treatment of Travellers and Gypsies, ethnic minority groups who traditionally lived nomadic lives and who experience everyday discrimination and racism. Dalits, Travellers, and their supporters are seeking to improve the conditions of marginalised people, and hashtags that draw attention to their situation a an important tool in this struggle. However other, more powerful groups have adapted the slogan in ways that uphold, rather than challenge, social norms. One such example is #BlueLivesMatter, which is a pro-police hashtag that originated in the US. Another example is #AllLivesMatter, which is usually counterposed against #BlackLivesMatter. While ostensibly concerned with social justice, the real effect of #AllLivesMatter is to divert attention away from the experiences of Black people and from challenges to the status quo.

These hashtags and actions show networks of solidarity, resistance and activism that, from local events, spread nationally and internationally, often through the use of social media. Localised social movements – like #BLM – become, in the era of social media induced diffusions, a global rage which crosses transnational boundaries, redefining their geographical influence and changing as they come into contact with other issues and geographies. Similarly, social media platforms owned and influenced by the affluent and the rich are being subverted for dissemination of ideas that threaten these structures. This could be in the form of making possible a

Figure 1.8 #DalitWomenFight Protest at the Dalit Women Fight Yatra in the US, 2015.

Source: Thenmozhi Sondararajan, Equality Labs.

political assertion, or allowing people to cherish and redraw aspirational geographies for themselves.

VI. CONCLUSION – MAKING BETTER LIVES POSSIBLE

This chapter shows that resistance, activism, and solidarity are often connected: a feeling of being united can give communities courage to resist imposed change or to mobilise to bring about new changes. And resistance, activism and solidarity are often associated with communities who are less powerful or marginalised, as they offer collective ways to challenge dominant and structural power. We demonstrated this through a range of examples, from the Niyamraja and Farmers' protests in India demonstrating community and resistance, to the activism of the Repeal movement in Ireland and the local, national, and global solidarities that emerged from the Black

Lives Matter movement. These examples provide many positive instances of change, but there is always more work to be done. For this reason, it is important to critically reflect on these campaigns in order to acknowledge the sacrifices that may have been made to achieve a particular goal. It is important to recognise that people may have been left out or marginalised in discussions, poster campaigns, and policies, and that they need to be heard in ways that disrupt discussions of 'success'. Understanding success critically then enables both celebration and reflection to develop on what has been created, but also acknowledges loss, limitation, and ongoing injustices.

More broadly, this chapter demonstrates that people are rising and resisting. These acts of resistance could be limited to a localised geography, or could respond to a global crisis affecting the world. They could use conventional modes of protests or creative strategies of organisation and mobilisation through the deployment of digital technologies. As an example, many developing world states, during the COVID-19 pandemic, failed to provide the requisite material and health resources. Faced with this, people raised help, support and resources using Instagram, WhatsApp and other social media platforms. Oxygen cylinders, food supplies, medicines, and care packages were fundraised and supplied to different places and people, such as those who were not given access to government care. This produced new (even if short lived) networks, channels and geographies of care and solidarity. In this way, resistance, activism, and solidarity refashioned the worlds we know of, the connections we make and communities we form; showing us the possible worlds that can be. For change to happen, we need to work with others to help make better lives possible, through acts of resistance and solidarity in and across space and place. The words of Dhiren Borisa sum this up:

> Often silenced!
> we are told, and repeatedly,
> we cannot speak.
> That our words do not hold matter.
> That we do not own merit.
> That they speak better,
> better than us.
> for us.
> That we shall be spoken about

60 MAKING SOCIAL CHANGE POSSIBLE

in words
we can never claim.
In the language of the oppressor
where we are chained,
our tongues, but slit.
But what happens
when we speak,
undoing this silence?
We become free.
We burst their myths.
We write ourselves into histories.
of our doings.
our resistance.
our victories.

NOTES

1 Poem by Tamil poet Sukirtharani published in "Wild Words" an anthology of four Tamil poets translated by Lakshmi Holmström and published by Harper Collins, 2015.

2 Indigenous persons in India with roots in the land that pre-existed the settlers who later rearranged the social order into hierarchical, violent, and discriminatory caste groups. Adivasis are not a homogenous group. However, in 1950 they were classified as Scheduled Tribes in the year 1950 to allow for affirmative action policies.

3 Excerpt from Jacinta Kerketta's first poetry collection "Angor" meaning Ember published by Adivaani, Kolkata in 2016 and translated into English by Bhumika Chawla D'Souza.

4 Borde, R. and B. Bluemling (2021) "Representing indigenous sacred land: The case of the Niyamgiri movement in India". *Capitalism Nature Socialism* 32(1): 68–87. https://doi.org/10.1080/10455752.2020.1730417.

5 Roe V Wade was overturned by the US Supreme Court in 2022.

6 The marriage bar was in place until 1973 but women were removed from employment after marriage beyond this point.

7 The most recent estimate of the population of India is around 1.5 billion. See www.worldometers.info/world-population/india-population/.

8 Bhowmick, N. (2021) "'I cannot be intimated. I cannot be bought'. The women leading India's farmers protests". *Time*, 4 March. Available online at https://time.com/5942125/women-india-farmers-protests/.

9 Taylor, K.-Y. (2016) *From #BlackLivesMatter to Black Liberation.* Chicago: Haymarket Books, p. 176.

10 The Movement for Black Lives (M4BL) (2023) *About Us*. Available online at https://m4bl.org/about-us/.
11 Weffer, S. E., R. Dominguez-Martinez and R. Jenkins (2018) "Taking a knee". *Contexts* 17(3): 66–68. https://doi.org/10.1177/1536504218792529.
12 Houghteling, C. and P. A. Dantzler (2020) "Taking a knee, taking a stand: Social networks and identity salience in the 2017 NFL protests". *Sociology of Race and Ethnicity* 6(3): 396–415. https://doi.org/10.1177/233264 9219885978.
13 www.nytimes.com/2020/05/31/us/george-floy dinvestigation.html#:~: text=They've%20kept%20Floyd%20lying,banned%20by%20most%20 police%20departments.
14 Della Porta, D., A. Lavizzari and H. Reiter (2022) "The spreading of the Black Lives Matter movement campaign: The Italian case in cross-national perspective. *Sociological Forum* 37(3): 700–721. https://doi.org/10.1111/socf.12818.
15 Leib, J. I. (2002) "Separate times, shared spaces: Arthur Ashe, Monument Avenue and the politics of Richmond, Virginia's symbolic landscape". *Cultural Geographies* 9(3): 286–312. https://doi.org/10.1191/147447400 2eu250oa.
16 Steinberg, P. (2022) "Blue planet, Black lives: Matter, memory, and the temporalities of political geography". *Political Geography* 96. https://doi. org/10.1016/j.polgeo.2021.102524.

FURTHER READING

BOOKS

Blunt, A. and J. Wills (2000) *Dissident Geographies: An Introduction to Radical Ideas and Practice*. Harlow: Longman.
Routledge, P. (2017) *Space Invaders: Radical Geographies of Protest*. London: Pluto Press.
Routledge, P., and A. Cumbers (2009) *Global Justice Networks: Geographies of Transnational Solidarity*. Manchester: Manchester University Press.
Soundararajan, T. (2022) *Trauma of Caste: A Dalit Feminist Meditation on Survivorship, Healing, and Abolition*. Berkeley, CA: North Atlantic Books.

JOURNALS

ACME: An International E-journal for Critical Geographies. Available online at https://acme-journal.org/index.php/acme
Antipode: A Radical Journal of Geography. Available online at https://onlinelibrary. wiley.com/journal/14678330 and at https://antipodeonline.org/about-the-journal-and-foundation/a-radical-journal-of-geography/

ARTICLES

The Combahee River Collective Statement (1977) Available online at www.blackpast.org/african-american-history/combahee-river-collective-statement-1977/

Crenshaw, K. (1991) "Mapping the margins: Intersectionality, identity politics, and violence against women of color". *Stanford Law Review*, 43(6), 1241.

Rich, A. (1984) "Notes towards politics of location". In *Blood, Bread, and Poetry: Selected Prose 1979–1985*. New York: W.W. Norton, pp. 210–231. Available online at https://genius.com/Adrienne-rich-notes-toward-a-politics-of-location-annotated

Sullivan, C. (2018) "Majesty in the city: Experiences of an Aboriginal transgender sex worker in Sydney, Australia". *Gender, Place and Culture*, 25(12), 1681–1702.

OTHER RESOURCES

BLM Website. Available online at https://blacklivesmatter.com/
Foil Vedanta Website. Available online at www.foilvedanta.org

GEOGRAPHIES OF DIFFERENCE

I. INTRODUCTION

Difference is a fundamental part of how we understand and organise ourselves, our societies, and the places and spaces we inhabit. To understand what we mean by difference, it's important to begin with identities, which refer to how we see ourselves and others, and how others see us.

As we seek to understand identities, we create differences from others in order to define who we are, what we like, and how we live (Box 2.1). Consider who you see as different to you: where are these differences noticeable to you? Think about where you go and where you don't go: where do you feel different? Difference in itself is not negative. However, it becomes harmful when it is used to create hierarchies of identities, for example seeing men as superior to women. Where difference is not noticed or felt, we can recognise privilege in being part of what is considered 'normal' and therefore unmarked. This can be associated with particular identities and bodies. In the context in which the authors, Kath and Mary, are located, white, heterosexual, able-bodied identities are the norm. For the authors Dhiren and Niharika, upper caste, Hindu, heterosexual, able-bodied identities are the norm. When we think about identities, it's also important to recognise their connection to bodies, because bodies can be core to how identities and differences are understood (Box 2.2).

DOI: 10.4324/9781003266877-3

BOX 2.1 IDENTITIES

Identities are the markers we give to the social differences and similarities that we have with others. The markers that are used are varied: they could include gender or sexuality; age or dis-abilities; race, ethnicity, or caste; nationality or religion, or any combination of these. Identities are formed both in terms of how we understand ourselves in relation to other people and how we are read by other people – both in alignment with our self-understanding and/or in contradistinction to it. How we understand ourselves and how people understand us can vary depending on where we are. Some aspects of our identities will matter in some spaces, and not in others.

BOX 2.2 BODIES

Discussions of identities can neglect the bodies that constitute them. Yet the material fleshiness of bodies can be core to difference – such as fat bodies. Fat activists, particularly in the Global North, have shown that fat bodies are excluded on the basis of their physicalities, with tables too close together in restaurants or fixed tables/chairs that are built with the presumption of specific body sizes. This can also be gendered, classed, and racialised where certain bodies are more easily seen as 'fat' and ridiculed, excluded (including from accessing life-saving medical services), and made to be and feel out of place.

Social groupings, classifications, bodies, and how they are hierarchised are not isolated from each other but are interconnected. This has been discussed by Black Feminists through the lens of intersectionality (Box 2.3). At first, intersectionality was used to draw attention to problems with feminism, specifically that feminism claimed to be universal but was in fact centring the experiences of white women. Kimberlé Crenshaw argued that it is important to see how gender intersects with race, resulting in very specific experiences of discrimination for Black women.[1] Since its introduction, intersectionality has spread to other contexts, and is now used to show how different grounds of identity, in different places, give rise to different forms of marginalisation and inequality.

BOX 2.3 INTERSECTIONALITY

The idea of singular identities was criticised by legal scholar Kimberlé Crenshaw who argued that Black women were both women and Black in ways that made their identities and lives different from those who were white women or Black men. The term intersectionality since then travelled across the globe and is directly associated with racialised and caste-ed intersections, as they engage with class, sexualities, dis/ability, religion, as well as other social differences. Multiple marginalisation refers to the ways in which identities and social locations combine to discriminate and oppress specific groups/people. Many such experiences of discrimination and oppression can persist over generations and hundreds of years, but they are not the same everywhere.

Social geographers have spent a lot of time discussing difference and what it means for the places we live in. Underpinning the social geographies approach is that how we are created as different depends on where we are, and where we are is an important part of how difference is made. Therefore, difference is dependent not only on *who* you are, but *where* you are. This leads to individuals or groups feeling 'in place' or 'out of place' on the basis of bodies, identities and difference (Box 2.9). Think, for example, how racialised bodies can be read differently depending on where we are, and who is making those places. However, it is not only people who are made through difference. Difference is made through places, and places are made through difference. Social geographers show how places are created through seeing one place as 'better than' another. The differences between how places are seen and hierarchised have implications for those who inhabit or use them. Some places are seen as 'better' than others and people are treated differently if they can access them: think of first class/economy class in travel for example. When we consider this in terms of neighbourhoods, schools, workplaces and so on, it means that the people in and of certain places are seen differently and their lives are affected by this.

Social geographers also draw attention to spaces of difference. If we associate difference with being different from the norm, then spaces of difference allow those who are marginalised to feel safe and comfortable, at least temporarily. From this perspective, spaces of differences could include gay clubs or restaurants catering to migrants, or quiet rooms for people with autism. These spaces of difference can offer respite and community. For marginalised communities, feeling welcome and being able to feel somewhat safe somewhere can be life-saving. An alternate understanding is linked to capitalism, as transnational corporations and city leaders seek to sell difference. For example, when McDonalds opened in India, it replaced its usual beef patty with an '*aloo tikki*', a potato-based patty (Figure 2.1). In this way, a transnational corporation represented itself as sensitive to the local context, while mostly replicating practices that are globally familiar. City leaders also seek to appropriate spaces of differences as a way of marking a city as cosmopolitan, and thus attractive to global capital (Figure 2.2).

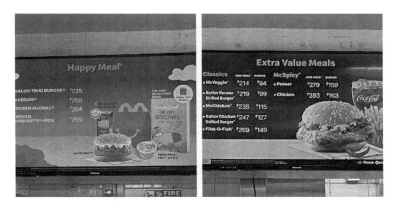

Figure 2.1 Photo of McDonalds Menu in New Delhi Including *aloo tikki* (Potato Patty) Burger and Butter Chicken Burger to Adapt to North Indian Tastebuds.

Source: Author's photographs.

Figure 2.2 Photo of The Irish House Pub at Indira Gandhi International Airport New Delhi on 14 February 2023.

Source: Author's photograph.

Bodies, identities, and spaces are influenced by, and in turn influence, our understanding of difference. Which differences matter varies locally, regionally, nationally, and transnationally. Social geographers seek to show how difference works to separate and divide people and places, defining where people can and can't be. This, in turn, influences the social, which is affected by and through where we are and what we do. In this chapter, we look at difference – specifically the varied geographies of difference – in a selection of case studies that highlight how difference is created, maintained, and challenged in and through space and place. We first look at how knowledge about difference is created, with examples from the discipline and practice of geography. We next look at gated communities as a way to maintain difference through geographies of inclusion and exclusion. In the final section, we expand our understanding of the geographies of difference to include the more-than-human, including both animals and things.

II. WHERE AND HOW KNOWLEDGE IS MADE

We have seen that social geographers are interested in the ways in which differences between places and people are created. This is the process of creating knowledge about places and people (Box 2.4). In this section, we look at the different roles geographers have played in creating knowledge, through formal and community organisations.

> ### BOX 2.4 CREATING KNOWLEDGE
>
> It is important to recognise that knowledge is actively created by people, rather than being a series of unchanging 'facts' that exist to be observed. Because knowledge is created, the role of science is to explain, experiment, explore, and refine knowledge. This perspective requires that we examine the role of the scientist – the creator of knowledge. Often, scientists are presented as people who are 'objective' and 'neutral', whose socio-cultural location and physical attributes do not matter to the questions being researched. In this sense, some people are seen as having 'no body' and thus able to take an unbiased and neutral stand. This is in contrast to those who are understood to be 'biased' because of their inability to stand outside of themselves and their bodies. However, once we understand all knowledge as created, we can question how knowledge is made, by who, and to what ends. We can then see the limitations of this knowledge and how it might serve particular groups, rendering others and their forms of knowledge 'unknown' and at times unrecognisable.

The discipline of Geography has played a part in creating social and spatial differences across the world. This is perhaps most apparent when looking at professional organisations such as the Royal Geographical Society (RGS). The RGS was established in 1830, as an organisation for men to go on expeditions to 'discover' other places and map them as part of the British colonial project. This work helped to support colonialism and imperialism, and it also served to construct social and spatial differences. As David Livingstone wrote in his history of the discipline: "Geography was not merely engaged in *discovering* the world; it was *making* it".[2]

The world that was made by explorers, and by the RGS and other professional organisations, was a world of hierarchies. Those hierarchies were based on subjective assessments about both people and places, and they described and reinforced both racial and spatial differences. We have mentioned the RGS, but it is just one of a wide number of geography societies and organisations that played an active role in this process, including societies in different parts of Britain, France, Germany and Portugal. The *National Geographic*, a magazine published by National Geographic Society in the US from 1888 onwards, also served to popularise a hierarchical view of the world, with the US at the top and other places – particularly in Africa, Asia, and Latin America – presented as more backward. The idea of Britain or the US as the centres that 'find out' about other places is key to how geography as a discipline, and more broadly knowledge about places and people, has been framed. The film *Paddington* includes a scene that reflects this work. Paddington Bear and Mr Brown go to the (fictional) Geographers' Guild to find out about an expedition the Guild funded to "darkest Peru". The receptionist describes just how much information the Guild has gathered about other places: "there are over two million letters, diaries and artefacts up in our archive", she says in exasperation when Mr Brown asks if he can have a look. The Geographers' Guild was modelled on the RGS, and this scene shows how knowledge about other places was gathered and stored as part of the process of making these places for the benefit of imperialism. The extensive knowledge gathered by the RGS and other professional organisations was used to map the world and create hierarchies of places based on subjective assessments about levels of 'development' or 'civilisation'. Organisations such as the RGS become arbiters of truth in certain places/times, defining who is an 'expert' and ensuring that their particular knowledge is recognised, valued, shared, and developed. In the process, Indigenous communities are marginalised and their knowledge is discounted.

Knowledge is thus made somewhere. It is linked to intersectional power relations including those related to coloniality, gender, race, caste, and age. It is not only who creates knowledge that matters, it also matters where knowledge is created. Terms such as 'East' and 'West' or 'Orient' and 'Occident' have shaped geographical imaginations which, as the scholar Edward Said points out, are not natural but *naturalised*. Said conceptualised this as Orientalism, as a stereotypical and over-generalised way to form knowledge about places and people who were colonised. Spatial knowledge such as 'East and West', 'Occident and Orient', or even 'Global North and Global South' cannot therefore be taken for granted (Box 2.5). Instead, we need to examine them critically to understand what purpose such geographical binaries serve. Thinking with the concept of Orientalism is to think geographically. To think geographically is also to understand the geographical ambitions of colonialism.

BOX 2.5 ORIENTALISM

Orientalism was a concept created by Edward Said in 1978 to point to the geographical imaginings and production of the 'non-west', especially Asia and the Middle East, by those in Europe and the US. Said showed how various cultural artefacts produced by colonial powers in the eighteenth and nineteenth centuries – for example paintings, literature and travelogues – helped create static stereotypes of the 'Orient'. This served to ultimately portray people living in this region as 'backward', 'uncivilised' and at times dangerous. They were/are also exoticised as strange others, both desired and detested.

However, official and hierarchical knowledge about places and their differences has been challenged by social geographers in recent years. The Detroit Geographical Expedition Institute is often used as an example. Founded in 1968 by academic geographer William Bunge and Black rights activist Gwendolyn Warren, the Institute sought to highlight social and racial inequalities and injustices in the city. In contrast to 'official' knowledge creation, Bunge and Warren trained people in the community in geographic methods and sent them on field expeditions into the city to map and identity spatial injustice. Such critical cartographies highlighted the spatialities of racial segregation, poverty, and inequalities in access to education and resources. They created maps looking at where babies were bitten by rats and where 'commuters run over Black children', all indicating the ways in which difference was manifest and affected people's material and social lives. However, the broader power dynamics of knowledge creation in Geography about people and places is also evident here. Bunge – an older white man – is credited as one of the founders of (US) critical and radical geographies. The crucial role and contribution of Warren – a younger Black woman – is often overlooked or sidelined. The work of Warren, Bunge and other members of the Institute was ground-breaking (Figure 2.3). It democratised maps by training people in the tools needed to make them, and thus made it possible for people who were directly affected to create their own representations of place.

The insights of Edward Said and the work of the Detroit Geographical Expedition Institute draw attention to the power that is inherent in the making of knowledge about a particular place and

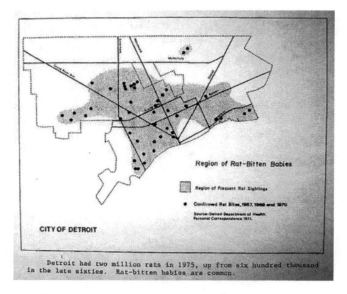

Figure 2.3 Bunge's Map of Detroit 'Rat Bitten Babies', 1975.

Source: William Bunge and Robert Bordessa. *The Canadian Alternative: Survival, Expedition, and Urban Change*. (Toronto: York University 1975), p. 326.

Available on: https://jacket2.org/commentary/william-bunge-dgei-radical-cartography, used under creative commons licence – Attribution-NonCommercial-ShareAlike 3.0 Unported (CC BY-NC-SA 3.0) (https://creativecommons.org/licenses/by-nc-sa/3.0/).

its people. Critically interrogating these power relations is crucial to the process of decolonising the discipline of Geography (Box 2.6). Geographers interested in decolonisation have focused on showing how and where difference is created, and the impacts of this. To continue with the example outlined, geographers have shown how the emergence of the Royal Geographical Society is informed by, and in turn reinforces racialised power relations. This, then, questions the objectivity of how geographic knowledge is made. Similar to the insistence on local knowledge that underpinned work in Detroit, geographers interested in decolonising the discipline may be interested in the 'Indigenous' perspective to a place. For example, if you are currently living in a settler colony like the US or Canada or Australia, then you may ask yourself:

- Are you part of a 'settler' community or part of a people who have longer ancestral and spiritual ties to the land?
- How would you map your ties to your land over a few generations if you were from an Indigenous background (e.g., Native American, First Nations, or Aboriginal Australian); from a settler background; or from a background of forced migration (e.g. slave, indentured labour or convict)?

The answers emerging from such questioning will reveal that settlers with economic and military resources as well as technical tools create knowledge about land and place while they dispossess those who are indigenous to the place or marginalise those who were forcibly moved to the place. This type of questioning is a practice in decolonisation.

BOX 2.6 DECOLONISING GEOGRAPHY

Calls to decolonise Geography emphasise the colonial roots of the discipline and how these continue to shape the practice of geography today. Advocates argue for radical change to structures and institutions that are based on or have benefited from colonial domination, and for the centring of the perspectives of those who have been racially othered and marginalised by colonialism.[3]

GEOGRAPHIES OF DIFFERENCE   **73**

Within the discipline of social geography, certain topics and approaches are seen as central and celebrated. Other places, concerns, and modes of enquiry are considered more marginal. In the language of social geography, often the marginal is expressed through terms such as 'regional'. That is, those forms of knowledge that are typically outside the Anglo-American context are usually termed regional with little or no theoretical relevance to explain global processes. Social geographies are thus located and created in and through Anglo-American lives and the socials created in these places, with lives outside the Anglo-American world as regional. Naming this shows that place-based patterns of inclusion, hierarchisation and exclusions are also made through how we make knowledge. The process of counter-topography is helpful here, as it seeks the unexpected ways in which places are connected (Box 2.7). The unexpected nature of the connection comes from how we have created knowledge within Geography and within social geography.

BOX 2.7 COUNTERTOPOGRAPHY

Countertopography questions the ways in which official stories about mapping and places are created, and seeks to make new and different knowledges. First developed by feminist geographer Cindi Katz, it draws attention to how places we think of as different are in fact connected because of their relationship to broader structures of power.

However, questioning how knowledge has been created can be twisted into 'post-truth' landscapes (Box 2.8). In post-truth landscapes, there is an unwillingness to rely on, or even believe, scientific evidence. Instead, the charge of 'fake news' can be applied to almost anything that a person, group, or organisation disagrees with. 'Fake news' is often linked to 'global elites', mainstream media, and 'woke' academics, and asserts that knowledge that comes from these sources is inevitably 'biased' and therefore untrue. This bias can be related to funding sources or political leanings, such as progressive approaches that question hierarchies of power. Post-truth landscapes use critiques of knowledge that geographers and others have developed as a key part of our scholarly/scientific advancement. As we have shown, social geographers and others have demonstrated that all knowledge is constituted, and highlighted the structures of power that underpin the creation of knowledge. However, rather than dismissing knowledge as 'fake news', social geographers interrogate its production in relation to place by asking where it was made, how it is used, and for/by whom. Subjecting what we know and can know to these place-based critiques creates more and better knowledge that has the potential to make our worlds better, by refusing to rely on one truth from one place and one positioning.

> ## BOX 2.8 POST-TRUTH
>
> Post-truth is where evidence and facts are queried to the point that they are negated. This can be seen in public, social media and other discussions where arguments are based on pre-existing beliefs and feelings rather than empirical evidence, grounded in research.

III. GATED COMMUNITIES: INEQUALITIES, INCLUSION, AND EXCLUSION

Gated or walled communities are housing complexes with strictly controlled access. They are a global phenomenon, predominantly but not exclusively located in urban areas. People have been creating and policing gated communities for centuries. An early and widespread example is city walls, which were used to separate the population within the walls from those outside. City walls were used for defensive purposes, for enhancing wealth and power, and for keeping the urban population separate from people and practices who were deemed unsafe or undesirable. In today's world, gated communities also work to separate those who live in them from people outside. The 'other' to gated communities is usually then understood as 'dangerous', 'disgusting', and less worthy than those who can use these communities freely and feel as though they 'belong'. In this way, bodies are defined as 'in' or 'out' of place through the segregation of space (Box 2.9). This results in geographies of inclusion/exclusion based on who people are and their desirability in a particular gated community (Box 2.10).

BOX 2.9 IN PLACE/OUT OF PLACE

Whereas exclusion is usually considered in terms of visible exclusions such as segregation or ghettoisation, there are also less visible ways in which difference is made to be exclusionary. This can be as subtle as a particular look given to someone who is 'out of place' or it can take more overt forms such as violence. Making people feel out of place and unwelcome is often created through what is seen as 'common sense' or 'normal' to a place. Those who don't fit are reminded of this through subtle or overt noticing or confrontations. In contrast, those who do fit are not subjected to being noticed, commented on, or challenged. These acts of noticing, commenting, and challenging create and recreate place by defining and reinforcing who is in/out of place. As an example, male/female toilets have certain common-sense norms about who fits, often based on visual assessments of gender. Who is 'seen' as a woman is more important than who identifies as one in these common-sense assumptions, and this in turn influences how people are confronted in these spaces.

BOX 2.10 GEOGRAPHIES OF INCLUSION/EXCLUSION

Geographies of difference started by looking at who was excluded from particular places. This includes physical exclusion from particular spaces, such as gated communities. It also includes those denied rights to the city, like access to public space. Social geographies consider the grounds on which people are excluded, such as class, caste, gender, racialisation, dis/abilities, sexualities, and age. In contrast, geographies of inclusion focus on who feels included in particular places, while recognising that inclusion and exclusion are mutually constituted.

Communities are gated in a variety of ways and for a wide range of reasons. Blakely and Snyder, in their study of gated communities in the US, identified three main types of gated communities. The first is lifestyle: for example, retirement communities or communities built around a particular leisure activity, such as golf. In these communities, people are included or excluded on the basis of social characteristics like age or leisure pursuits. Known as retirement homes, senior living, or simply gated communities, housing facilities for seniors promise to offer secure, independent living in comfortable premises, usually outside of metropolitan centres, such as in the Glades in Florida and Western Cape in South Africa. Urban studies scholars often read these communities as clustering around age in the suburbs, reproducing patterns of racial homogeneity and spatial differentiation. Such age-based communities, while securing lives of elderly communities, also increase place-based racial and class segregation. The second is prestige. These are usually connected to wealth and privilege and status, with people admitted on the basis of their income, capital, or fame. Gated communities like these can be related to housing or leisure pursuits where access is exclusive to those who can afford access or have particular notoriety to live or socialise in these spaces. The third is security, where people are included or excluded on the basis of residence which is linked to a fear of outsiders.

The materialities of gated communities are diverse (Figure 2.4).[4] They can include physical barriers or boundaries: gates, fences, bollards, or inaccessible hedges or vegetation. They can include signs to indicate ownership – 'private property' – or to exert control over behaviour, for example asking visitors to report to an office. They can include checkpoints that are policed by guards, and/or security grills or surveillance technology, such as security cameras or drones, monitored on or off site. In extreme situations, gated communities can have armed guards or armed response teams. Within gated communities, residents are often subject to stringent controls, for example over how their residence should look or what they are allowed to do. Contemporary gated communities may have been originally linked with the US and South Africa, but they have spread rapidly, particularly to places with significant social and spatial inequality. Recently, gated communities have been described as

Figure 2.4 Gated Communities in Dublin, Ireland.
Source: Authors' photos.

the 'new normal' in Latin America,[5] and have become significantly more common across Asia and Africa.

Gated communities have been likened to the fortresses of the past that sought to protect settlements from invasions. This notion of 'invasion' is key to the geographies of difference embodied in gated communities. Those who transgress into spaces where they do not belong, for example travelling communities who move into areas that are gated to exclude them, are often read as out of place and 'polluting' what is seen as 'pure' space. Being out of place takes multiple forms. In semi-private commercial centres like shopping malls/centres certain bodies are seen as 'normal' and 'in place', whereas others are subject to surveillance. This can be seen where security guards follow young people of colour in shopping centres in Britain or Ireland, watching their behaviours in ways that others are not subject to. Their bodies define them as different and potentially dangerous to (often white) managers/security guards. These gated communities operate without physical gates. Other examples include suburban areas which can be seen as gated not through physical barriers but through expectations about who should, and should not, live there. When those expectations are transgressed, new geographies of difference are created. An example is white flight, when white people move out of an area that is becoming more ethnically diverse. This movement shows how areas become defined by who is considered in or out of place, even if there are no material signs in the form of gates or fences.

The practice of protecting gated communities from pollution took a complex and disturbing turn in urban centres in India during the COVID-19-induced lockdown. Various Dalit groups, who are required to scavenge and clean by a tradition decided by upper castes over hundreds of years, were claimed to be carriers of the coronavirus and kept out of gated communities, even when they were required to pick the garbage from select places in the communities. This can also be seen in the experiences of people who are homeless, when city spaces are 'cleaned up' with physical structures put in place to stop their access or sleeping (for example hard metal objects on benches so it is not possible to lie down on them, see Figure 2.5). There is also policing of bodies within gated communities including along intersectional lines of class, race, and caste that goes beyond who can access the place. Even where those who are perceived as different are allowed to enter, certain bodies are made to be 'out of place'. In the US, Black people have been challenged and in extreme cases killed for entering residential gated communities that they were entitled to be in (for example, because they lived or worked there, or were visiting people or using public facilities). Their bodies read as out of place and dangerous, and they become other to the place itself. In this way, the racialised classed norm of the place is violently enforced. Gating can also be practised by a cluster of nation-states. Scholars have argued that the EU works to secure easy mobility and migration for some groups of migrants and not others. The EU makes it easy for EU citizens to move and live within EU borders. It is much more difficult for those who are not from the EU to move to the EU to live, unless they have particular skills or qualities. For example, people from outside the EU who are trained medical professionals or software engineers are often seen as 'skilled migrants' and given privileged access to the EU. In contrast, it is often very difficult for a person without specific specialised training to be admitted to the EU, particularly if they are a citizen of a country that requires a visa to even visit the EU. In this situation, we can see why the EU is sometimes described as 'Fortress Europe'. Social geographers are interested in the racial, ethnic, and class considerations that go into the construction of 'outsiders', while trying to figure out how a cluster of nation-states can also practice sorting difference through economic and immigration policies.

GEOGRAPHIES OF DIFFERENCE 79

Figure 2.5 DART Benches in Dublin that Cannot be Used for Sleeping on and are not Under Shelter to Protect People from Rain.

Source: Authors' Photo.

Gated communities have long been controversial as they enclose space for an elite few. In addition to residential enclaves and compounds, gating can also be used to prevent access to other resources or facilities. For example, leisure facilities such as golf clubs sometimes close off vast tracts of land for exclusive use that once might have been open to the public and within public ownership. In the south of Ireland, for example, the public pathways at the Old Head of Kinsale were enclosed for a golf course only accessible to those who could pay and wanted to play golf. Gated communities are associated with social prestige, creating differences between a lesser 'them' and a better 'us' physically in the landscape through who has access and who does not. Creating literal walls around particular social groups creates and further entrenches the inequitable distribution of housing, public space, leisure facilities, and so on, deepening spatial divisions. Segregation of urban spaces is a key outcome of gated communities, particularly when they proliferate in residential areas, retail centres, and public space. Gating then is a specific form

GEOGRAPHIES OF DIFFERENCE

of bordering, where either physical walls or social borders create hierarchised differences. Places are made through the processes of bordering and in turn the process and the places make social differences that define people's identities and lives by being included/excluded, in place/out of place.

IV. MORE-THAN HUMAN GEOGRAPHIES: ANIMALS, TECHNOLOGIES, AND NON-HUMAN SOCIAL LIVES

Difference does not just refer to humans. To understand the 'social' of social geographies, it is important to acknowledge that difference also refers to the animals and other 'things' that make up our lives. Social geographers recognise that human beings live not only among themselves but also with animals, and with and through technologies. Thus, more-than-human geography sub-fields have emerged, including animal geographies and post-humanism (Box 2.11 and Box 2.12). Those who look at more-than-human geographies contest the division between humans and non-humans, and question if human agency (that is the ability to do things, make choices, determine life chances) is dependent on non-humans, including animals?

BOX 2.11 MORE-THAN-HUMAN GEOGRAPHIES

More-than-human geographies explore how human-animals-things relate to each other to create our society. It sees social lives as not just made by humans, but also created through *more-than-human relations*, things, and beings with whom we co-exist. This refuses the primacy of humans as the most important (and often seen as the sole) aspect of social relations, instead understanding the complex entanglements between humans/non-humans, what is termed trans-species theory. This approach is challenging politically, practically, and ethically because it decentres the human in the production of lives and asks for attention to be paid to how non-human life forms (as well as things) also have agency in how social relations and lives are made. This means that places are made not only by humans but also by the animals and objects that make and occupy these places. We can't understand contemporary human geography without the more-than-human. Equally, more-than-human understandings need spatial engagements.

BOX 2.12 POST-HUMANISM

Post-humanism asks us to consider the relationships between human and non-human differently. How humans and non-humans relate and encounter each other is key to how we make space and create difference in and through them. This has clear implications not only in thinking about the social, but also in doing everyday lives, as animal geographies show.

One of our early academic understandings of the relationship between humans and non-humans was provided by Donna Haraway. In an essay titled, "The Cyborg Manifesto", Donna Haraway used the concept of the cyborg to overcome the strict separations of human/animal/machine; a separation that is kept in place to argue for the superiority of the human in general and the male in particular. With the knowledge of evolutionary biology in Charles Darwin's *On the Origin of Species*, the Industrial Revolution (mid-eighteenth to early twentieth century) and the advancement in technology, boundaries between the human and the non-human cannot be understood as strictly delineated. This has implications for understanding difference. What is different from us may thus be part of us, and not inferior to us.

ANIMAL GEOGRAPHIES

Animal geographies explore the engagements between humans and animals, showing the ways in which human and non-human power relations and interactions play out: sometimes termed hybrid geographies (Box 2.13). Animals can often be seen as secondary, and inferior, to humans who are afforded primacy in discussions of social life, including the reconstitution of bodies, and relationships/family life. Whereas humans are understood to have agency, animals are seen as being subject to the will of humans. This feeds into and from our understandings of nature as pure/untouched/wild, in contrast to culture that is created by and for humans alone. Countering this is thinking that sees nature-culture as interlinked.

BOX 2.13 HYBRID GEOGRAPHIES/NATURE-CULTURE

Sarah Whatmore introduced the concept of hybrid geographies to name the ways that humans and non-humans are inter-dependent and form each other. She used 'nature' as an example of something that can be assumed to be formed through the non-human and opposite to culture. Whatmore challenges this assumption, arguing that nature-culture are mutually constituted, where nature makes human cultures through animals, trees, plants, and so on, and vice versa.

Understanding animals as living beings with rights can result in various responses from humans, including offering animals the status of 'people' to legally protect them from being killed. Vegetarianism and vegan practices and movements can also seek to challenge the hierarchy of human/non-human. Yet these practices are different in different places. In India, for example, a vegetarian diet can be read as pure in ways that reiterate Indian caste hierarchies. In this case, while seeking to readjust hierarchies between animals-humans, hierarchies of difference between social groups/castes are recreated through these practices. This points to the complexities of social relations that can resist easy binaries or solutions.

Pets and their role in various places is one example of how humans/non-humans interact to create societies, cultures, and power inequalities. When we talk of 'domestication', we usually consider pets as moving from 'wild animals' towards more domesticated companions. Yet, seeing pets as 'human companions' diminishes the ways in which pets and humans have co-evolved in terms of domestication to create forms of kinship and bonds. Humans and pets then can be seen as evolving together to create homes and families that challenge the primacy of the human in the relationship.

In some places and households, pets can be seen as family and kin. This can be in ways that are usually assumed to be reserved for human relationships that form families, particularly between couples or between a parent and a child. When we critically consider the hierarchical relationships that can be established between humans/non-humans, this differentiation is questionable. Why are human relationships more important and valued in certain places than relationships between humans and pets? Pet geographies then question the idea that social relations are solely human relations and instead draw attention to how human/non-human relationships are important for wellbeing and liveable lives. This broadens who counts as family/kin, and asks for an expanded use of spaces – such as social spaces, airplanes, and other forms of transport – that may have previously been used by humans only. There has also been an increase in the commercialisation of goods related to pets, particularly in places with declining human birth rates.

Pets are one dimension of animal geographies. Another dimension considers the role of technologies and things. This is clear if we consider agriculture, specifically farming, as created between plants/animals, technologies and humans to feed humans and non-human animals. Even in its most primitive form, farming requires tools to plant/harvest/make edible and it requires plants/animals and humans to make food. Throughout this process, across a range of scales, landscapes are reconstructed and relationships of power and co-dependencies are made. While all require the other to exist, it is the human who is usually afforded the hierarchical recognition of 'being a farmer'. Moreover, plants and animals are seen as being 'tamed' by the human, who in turn is understood as creating/controlling the technologies that make the activities of farming possible. Yet animals, plants, and tools also exceed this control.

GEOGRAPHY OF THINGS: CLOTHES

It is not only animals that need to be considered when exploring the broader contours of social landscapes and lives. Things are also critical to places, spaces, and lives. We might think technologies are only related to high-tech computerised and mediated social landscapes and cities (Box 2.14). These are important, but technology also relates to this book, its pages, what you are wearing, the pen you are writing with. Technologies are the things and processes that are central to how you make and create your everyday lives. Our social lives and the spaces/places that we live in and use are created by and through things. In other words, our social life has a materiality (Box 2.15). This means that it is not only abstract or related to words, discussions, and texts. It is also about our bodies and technologies, what we touch, feel, sense, and use.

BOX 2.14 TECHNOLOGIES

Technologies are skills, methods, techniques, and things that can be used for a purpose. They can be functional (for sitting/sleeping), they can be given specific meanings/emotions (for example family pictures), and they are crucial for how we engage with each other. Technologies are central to interactions between people/place and are key for understanding our social worlds across human/non-human divisions. Human lives do not exist outside technologies. Instead, we are created through how we develop, access, and use technologies. Access to technologies and the spaces created through diverse technologies can reiterate and recreate differences and hierarchies that lead to spaces of inclusion/exclusion. Technologies on their own cannot be seen as good or bad. It is in their use that meaning/value/import and differences are created and defined.

BOX 2.15 MATERIALITIES

Materialities are the physical stuff of life: what we can touch and feel and sense. For social geographers, this includes the places where we live, the food we eat, the maps we make: anything that has a physical or material presence.

The things that we use have a geography. They are made in one place under particular social relations: often inequitable relations of labour where the worker earns less than the value of the object created and the profit is transferred to the owner/shareholder. This can be seen for example in the clothing industry where workers in the Global South work for large multi-national corporations, designers, and 'fast-fashion' industries for salaries that are far below the value of the items that they produce. The things then move. In this movement we can see other power relations between states (who can trade where and with who, what taxes and customs are imposed). Consider the trade barriers around the European Union that allow some goods to enter and require all to meet European standards. These both facilitate some forms of trade, and limit others. The regulations seek to protect both EU consumers and EU businesses and, in doing so, they reiterate geopolitical powers. In our example, an item of clothing is labelled in terms of its composition and its place of origin (Figure 2.6).

When they arrive at their point of sale, clothes are then distributed and labelled within particular regulatory/commercial arrangements, underpinned by social relations. Clothes are often sold in ways that delineate gender (male/female sections of clothing shops or differentiated shops), style, price band, and other configurations. These are all spatial considerations: what clothes go where, for who, and for what bodies?

The end point of the commodity chain (the labour and processes that create a finished product) is the sale of the product from these shops. However, the clothes that we use have a life and meaning beyond the point of sale. Clothes are key to identities. What we wear, and where, speaks to who we are, and how we want to be seen. We make choices about the clothes we wear based on where

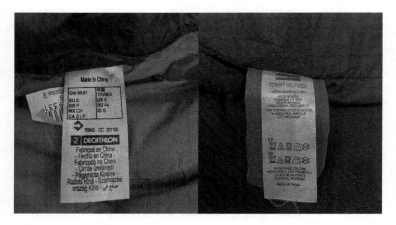

Figure 2.6 Clothes Labels Depicting Where They Were Produced.
Source: Authors' Photo.

86 GEOGRAPHIES OF DIFFERENCE

we are going to be, with different clothes for work and for going out, for formal occasions and for relaxing. All of these speak to how we make who we are, in part through what we wear. This is the case even when we seek to disrupt conventions by not wearing what is expected in particular spaces. The available choice of clothes, both in terms of fashion and what is considered desirable or acceptable, is influenced by social differences. Not all have the choice to wear various clothes and the implications of transgressing the norms of specific spaces range from strange looks to murder. For example, the consequences of dressing contrary to what is expected of your gender can be fatal. Not all have wardrobes of clothes to choose from. Even where expensive fashion labels can be afforded by an individual, they may not be desired. Clothes therefore work to define and create us, as we use them.

The life cycle of clothes is not complete even after their reuse. When clothes are discarded their social geographies remain important. In the US it is estimated that 85% of clothes end up in landfills or are burned. These clothes can take over 200 years to decompose. There is a move to increase the life cycle of clothes through reuse, such as giving clothes away or using charity shops or thrift stores to source second-hand clothing. However, there are huge environmental impacts in the creation, use and discarding of clothing. There can be little doubt that this relates to transnational relations of power that drive fashion industries (consider where the 'centres' of fashion are supposed to be: Paris, London, and New York) and pertains directly to local social geographies of identities, lifestyles, and consumption. Clothes then offer insights into the power relations that recreate differences between people, as well as how these differences are not only between humans but rely on the things and technologies. These differences make our social worlds through relations of power.

GEOGRAPHY OF THINGS: SMART CITIES

Alongside clothing, there are other technologies and things that define everyday lives for many of us. We carry, wear, and use technologies extensively through phones, computers, watches, glasses, and other digital devices that track, monitor, and connect us. These digital devices create, regulate, and normalise our social lives through our use of them, and their use of us. The spread of 'smart' technologies means that how we live, work, and socialise is networked in various ways. As with all technologies, digital 'smart' technologies are not inherently good or bad but, depending on how they are used, may result in or from inequalities, hierarchies, harm, and exploitation. Geographical differences are critical in the use of technologies, as is evident in the example of smart cities.

What smart cities are is not clear cut. The easiest way to introduce smart cities is to think about how information and communication technologies are used within cities to help solve urban problems, encourage economic growth and manage populations. Governments, businesses, security and emergency services, and other stakeholders are all involved in deploying technologies, like software, in smart cities, and in using the data generated to influence, change or control how cities are used. One example of smart city technologies is variable speed limits for traffic, where motorway speed limits are set by using cameras and traffic data to manage the flow of traffic and how fast it travels (Figure 2.7). This enables motorways to be safer and helps drivers to understand if there is congestion or an accident coming up so they can adjust their driving accordingly. There are significant urban transformations associated with smart cities. How the city is used and governed can be extensively changed through these technologies. This can reinforce already existing social and spatial differences and create new differences. For example, China used smart city technology to manage the movement of people during the COVID-19 pandemic using a government created and controlled app. The app was used to record details about COVID-19 test results, and to limit the use of public transport and other services to those who had not tested positive. When protests erupted during late 2022, this app was used to pinpoint who attended the protests and limited their movement by turning their health code red, meaning that they could not travel. In this way, smart city technology was used to create geographies of exclusion.

Because technologies have become normalised and an ordinary part of our everyday lives, they can obscure the power relations that shape our lives and our cities. Smart cities then engage and use power in various ways to create shared understandings of what

88 GEOGRAPHIES OF DIFFERENCE

Figure 2.7 Photo of Traffic Signals Outside Leicester City Railway Station on 24 February 2023.

Source: Authors' Photo.

is normal in ways that are inequitable. These can give power and control to some (often institutions like states, governments, and/ or businesses) in the form of data and surveillance, recreating neoliberal and/or state power relations that hierarchise differences

GEOGRAPHIES OF DIFFERENCE   89

between people. For example, geographer Ayona Datta demonstrates how in India smart cities can speed up lives, with things like faster transport, and quicker access to information.[6] Her research focused on young women who are marginalised both in terms of where they live in cities and their access to digital technologies. These women are extremely vulnerable to and aware of gendered violence due to hierarchies of power. This violence is mediated and somewhat mitigated against through security technologies that were put in place after a horrific, highly publicised attack of a woman on a bus in New Delhi. These technologies included a smart phone app and cameras in public spaces that were supposed to create smart safe cities. This sees violence as one-off events that can be stopped by technological interventions. It does not recognise the ways violence can be a part of people's 'normal' life, thus missing the realities of women's lives in New Delhi and elsewhere. The young women on the periphery of the city who Datta spoke to were managing things like deeply entrenched inequitable gendered home lives, and police inaction on violence against them. This meant that smart safe technologies did not address the key issues they faced as poor women.

What a smart city is, how it works, and what technologies are used differs across space and place. For example, smart cities in China are part of broader moves towards state economic development and population management. In Germany smart city technologies are deployed to make urban governance more efficient and make urban lives more sustainable. In the UK, smart cities are linked to marketisation and developing neoliberal opportunities to sell and commercialise data and the associated behaviours. However, despite these clear geographical differences, smart city technology advocates often seek to apply technology across cities without considering the needs of individual cities. This move towards flattening spatial differences may, in fact, reinforce existing differences or create new ones.

V. CONCLUSION: GEOGRAPHIES OF THE MARGINS

This chapter has explored geographies of difference. It did so in three key ways. First, it considered how knowledge about difference is created. It showed how hierarchies of people and place are created and contested, and highlighted the role of geographers in this

GEOGRAPHIES OF DIFFERENCE

process. Next, the chapter considered how difference is grounded through the creation of geographies of exclusion and inclusion. It focused in particular on gated communities but showed how the concept of gated communities has a long history and an extensive spatial reach. Finally, the chapter discussed more-than-human geographies. Through a range of different case studies – including animal geographies, clothes, and smart cities – the chapter moved us beyond relations between people to understand how social worlds, and thus social geographies, are both human and more-than-human.

These examples showed us how social geographers explore difference and the relations of power that create difference, differently in different places. Social geographers are interested in how and where differences are made, and how this creates hierarchies between people and places, as well as between humans and non-humans. Spatial differences emerge from and in turn shape hierarchies that privilege some and marginalise others, making some included/in place and others excluded/out of place. Examinations of difference have looked at exclusions that can be overt and visible and othering that can be far more subtle. Key to this is the deployment of power to create, use, occupy, and control spaces. Explorations of those who are excluded and exist on the margins have highlighted how discrimination and prejudice not only creates peoples' and animals' lives but also the spaces we live in.

NOTES

1 Crenshaw, K. (1993) "Mapping the margins: Intersectionality, identity politics and violence against women of color". *Stanford Law Review* 43: 1241–1300.
2 Livingstone, D. (1992) *The Geographical Tradition*. Malden, MA and Oxford: Blackwell, p. 168.
3 Esson, J., P. Noxolo, R. Baxter, P. Daley and M. Byron (2017) "The 2017 RGS-IBG chair's theme: Decolonising geographical knowledges, or reproducing coloniality?". *Area* 49(3): 384–388. https://doi.org/10.1111/area.12371.
4 Grant, J. and L. Mittelsteadt (2004) "Types of gated communities". *Environment and Planning B: Planning and Design* 31(6): 913–930. https://doi.org/10.1068/b3165.
5 Kostenwein, D. (2021) "Between walls and fences: How different types of gated communities shape the streets around them". *Urban Studies* 58(16): 3230–3246. https://doi.org/10.1177%2F0042098020984320.

GEOGRAPHIES OF DIFFERENCE **91**

6 Datta, A. (2020) "The 'Smart safe city': Gendered Time, speed, and violence in the margins of India's urban age". *Annals of the American Association of Geographers* 110(5): 1318–1334.

FURTHER READING

BOOKS

Bunge, W. (2011) *Fitzgerald: Geography of a Revolution*. Athens: University of Georgia Press.

Cresswell, T. (1996) *In Place/Out of Place: Geography, Ideology, and Transgression*. Minneapolis: University of Minnesota Press.

Gillespie, K., and R.-C. Collard (2017) *Critical Animal Geographies: Politics, Intersections, and Hierarchies in a Multispecies World*. London and New York: Routledge.

Said, E. W. (1978) *Orientalism*. New York: Vintage Books.

JOURNALS

Gender, Place and Culture. Available online at www.tandfonline.com/toc/cgpc20/current

ARTICLES

John, M. E. (2015) "Intersectionality: Rejection or critical dialogue?" *Economic and Political Weekly*, 50(33), 72–76.

Menon, N. (2015) "Is feminism about 'women'? A critical view on intersectionality from India." *Economic and Political Weekly*, 50(17), 37–44.

Raju, S. (2002) "We are different, but can we talk?" *Gender, Place and Culture: A Journal of Feminist Geography*, 9(2), 173–177.

OTHER RESOURCES

Borisa, D. (2020) *City and Sexuality: An Auto-Ethnographic Storytelling of Caste, Class and Queerness in Delhi*. Geography and You. Retrieved 29 March 2023, from www.geographyandyou.com/caste-and-class/city-and-sexuality-an-auto-ethnographic-storytelling-of-caste-class-and-queerness-in-delhi

Cook, I. (n.d.) *Follow the Things*. Follow the Things. Retrieved 28 February 2023, from www.followthethings.com/

3

GEOGRAPHIES OF PRECARITY

I. INTRODUCTION

"Lives are by definition precarious",[1] as Judith Butler wrote. We have no guarantees about how long our lives will be: they can end or be ended at any time. Because of this, being precarious – or precariousness – is an essential part of being human and being alive (Box 3.1). Precarity, in contrast, is not essential. Instead, it occurs when broader social structures create unequal life opportunities and conditions for certain people or groups of people. While all lives are precarious, not all people live in conditions of precarity, which refers to the insecure, temporary, and unguaranteed ways in which some lives are lived (Box 3.2). Precarity means being more prone to injury *caused* by socio-political and economic factors. People experience precarity because something is happening in the socio-structural context in which they reside. As Judith Butler explains:

> we cannot take for granted that all living humans bear the status of a subject who is worthy of rights and protections, with freedom and a sense of political belonging; on the contrary, such a

> ### BOX 3.1 PRECARIOUSNESS
>
> Precariousness is used to mean a general state where all human beings are prone to injury. That is, any human being can fall ill, be harmed, or die at any time. We are all precarious.

DOI: 10.4324/9781003266877-4

BOX 3.2 PRECARITY

Precarity describes people's insecure social and spatial positioning, and refers to those human beings and social groups who are more likely to be injured, ill, unemployed, or otherwise suffer/die. It was originally applied to people's work, with precarious work seen as offering little in the way of income or job security. Now, the term is used more widely to show how people's lives are destabilised and devalued in space and place. Some people are more precarious than others because of material and symbolic challenges that they have faced over generations or in one lifetime. These challenges may include a lack of access to resources (for example, food, water, housing, education, or employment) or statuses like citizenship or legal residence in a particular country.

status must be secured through political means, and where it is denied that deprivation must be made manifest.[2]

When geographers use the term precarity, they focus on *where* and *why* some lives are more insecure or temporary or unguaranteed than others. Initially, geographies of precarity focused on work, with a particular focus on how a free market economic ideology emphasises the need to reduce the security of workers. This has happened in several ways, including union-busting, employing people on short-term contracts, reducing pay, and disimproving conditions. Many of the people who teach you have been involved in disputes over these issues, such as the 'Four Fights' campaign about casualisation, inequality, low pay, and unsustainable workloads by UCU (University and College Union) in the UK. However, the geographies of precarity have moved beyond work to consider a variety of different ways in which lives are made more insecure. These structures include migration controls, legal protection, climate change, and differences such as gender, race, caste, sexuality, and ability. Geographies of difference are created and maintained through the actions of people and things, which in turn provide contexts for their lives. This makes life more insecure, temporary, and unguaranteed for some people and not others in ways that are not uniform and change through place and time. Consideration of whose lives matter and where, then, are intricately woven into the spatial and temporal fabric of our social worlds. For social geographers, precarity is a concept that can deepen our understanding of inclusion and exclusion by highlighting the material and symbolic conditions under which human beings try to make a living and survive.

When we think of geographies of precarity, we need to consider how lives are *made to be* different and less secure, and how these mechanisms vary between and across place and space. Drawing from what we have understood about geographies of difference developed in Chapter 2, this chapter expands to show where and how marginalisations, othering, and exclusions make people more precarious (Box 3.3). It emphasises the spaces and places where bodies are made more precarious, taking a scalar approach, where local and global issues are discussed. At a range of interconnected scales, we will see how human beings face growing insecurities and difficulties at work and finding secure housing, threats in public spaces and health, claims to citizenship and belonging in a nation, and displacements that arise from deteriorating environmental conditions. In this way, we show how the geographies of precarity are both influenced by, and in turn influence, hierarchical conceptualisations of difference(s) in place and space.

BOX 3.3 PRECARITY AND DIFFERENCE

Where precarity is related directly to social groups, difference plays a significant role in creating precarity. Differences that are hierarchised and normalised link directly to making lives more vulnerable to harm and make some lives less worthy compared to others. One's geographical location, caste, class, racial and ethnic background, gender, sexuality, able-bodiedness, age all play a role in constituting difference.

The concept of precarity also draws our attention to the broader politics of life and death: who lives, and who is 'allowed' to die. The term 'necropolitics' is used to describe the different ways in which people are 'allowed' to die, from war and violence to the depletion of resources and the failure to provide basic needs such as food, water, shelter, and healthcare (Box 3.4). Mbembe describes this as "the power to manufacture an entire crowd of people who specifically live at the edge of life, or even on its outer edge – people for whom living means continually standing up to death".[3] Space and place play a key role in who lives and who is allowed to die. Precarity is also linked to whose lives are deemed worthy of grieving with outpourings of support and sympathy (think of what happens when royalty in the UK die and the national mourning demanded) and whose lives are considered expendable (consider the crisis in the Mediterranean where bodies are being washed up on beaches and there is no state call for mourning).

BOX 3.4 NECROPOLITICS

The focus on precarity not only explores life but also the politics of death. Achille Mbembe discusses precarity and necropolitics through sovereignty; that is the ability to "exert one's control over mortality"[4] and to decide whether you and/or others can live or die. For Butler, who is worthy of a life is a political decision that creates precarity. Some lives are more grievable than others and thus protected in ways that others are not. Speaking of 'allowing people to die' is a way that necropolitics can be seen and is apparent in coverage of wars, refugee migrations and other ways that lives are made vulnerable.

A focus on precarity pushes us to consider where and whose lives are deemed worthy or entitled to a liveable life (Box 3.5). A liveable life is a life that is worth living, and we will see how some lives are deemed more worthy than others, leading to precarity for those lives that are considered less worthy. Precarity, therefore, also helps us move towards politics to see how we might remake spaces and places to enable those lives that are considered unworthy and therefore insecure move towards worthy and liveable lives.

> ## BOX 3.5 LIVEABLE LIFE AND PRECARITY
>
> Judith Butler popularised the term 'liveable life' by showing how some lives are more liveable than others. What makes life liveable is variable, dependent on social differences. The hierarchies of liveability depend on whose lives matter, where, and when. A life, whatever may be its substantive elements, is thus made liveable (or not) depending on what kind of material and symbolic resources it has access to. Some lives are more prone to precarity, making them less liveable (and less survivable) than others. The question then becomes, how might we make our life more liveable and less precarious?

In this chapter, we discuss the geographies of precarity in a few ways. We start by considering the broader structures of citizenship and belonging and show how access to citizenship and belonging may be restricted or denied, resulting in precarity for different groups of people. We discuss this in two different contexts: Denmark and India. We then discuss broader economic structures that cause precarity, such as the globalisation of corporations and the growth of digital labour. In the next section, we challenge precarity through the concept of liveable lives, looking at Pride and Grace Banu's example to show how people can come together to create more than bearable lives from marginalised positions. Asking for lives that are liveable opens possibilities beyond just surviving.

II. WHOSE LIVES MATTER, WHERE AND WHEN? CITIZENSHIP DEBATES IN DENMARK AND INDIA

Citizenship debates are prominent examples of understanding whose lives matter, where, and when. In formal terms, citizenship denotes membership of a community that is defined by a state. Being a citizen of a state confers rights on a person and comes with responsibilities. In this way, citizenship is both a legal status and a marker of social and political belonging (Box 3.6). Rights and responsibilities vary across different states. In some countries, such as the UK and the US, citizens have the right to vote but are not required to. In other countries such as Brazil and Australia, voting is compulsory for citizens, and those who do not vote may be fined. Citizens can also have protection from some states when visiting others, for example help with various issues from embassies and consulates, which may be more support than citizens of that place will get. For example, when the US withdrew from Afghanistan in 2021, European and American citizens were offered support to leave in ways that were not afforded to Afghan citizens.

BOX 3.6 BELONGING

For social geographers, belonging can be understood as a sense of attachment or connection to place, where that attachment or connection is an aspect of a person's identity. Social geographers often focus on particular scales or spaces of belonging, like 'home' or a neighbourhood or a state or nation-state. Conditions that are conducive to belonging, including supportive networks, can make people less vulnerable and precarious.

Citizenship is exclusive, and many people are not able to access citizenship in the places where they were born, live, or want to live. This exclusivity makes some people precarious because of their lack of access to citizenship: they may have no certainty that they can continue living in a place; they may have no rights to access public funds and/or services; they may be disenfranchised; or they may face restrictions in access to employment, housing, or the public sphere. When access to citizenship is enabled for some and restricted for others, it creates different possibilities for a liveable life through the rights granted by specific countries. Even when people have formal citizenship, this status may be mediated by several other factors such as race, ethnicity, or gender. For example, some citizens may get more protection from police or have more rights than others.

Citizenship is not equally distributed: some people have multiple citizenships, while others do not have citizenship and are considered 'stateless'. In general, people with citizenship of the state where they live have more rights than co-residents who do not have that citizenship. Some countries – such as the US, Argentina, Brazil, Cuba, Jamaica, and Tanzania – offer unrestricted birthright citizenship (sometimes called *jus soli*). This means that anyone born in the country is entitled to citizenship of that country. However, most countries do not offer unrestricted birthright citizenship. Instead, they might offer restricted birthright citizenship – for example, a parent needs to be legally resident for a certain number of years before birthright citizenship is granted. More commonly, countries award citizenship based on family ties (sometimes called *jus sanguinis*). For this, usually a parent needs to be a citizen in order for the child to be considered a citizen. There are also other routes to citizenship, such as naturalisation, where a person must meet a number of conditions and then is awarded citizenship of a country. These conditions vary across states, but could include passing language or citizenship tests, not having a criminal record, having a long period of legal residence and/or employment, and making a substantial payment.

Even when people are awarded citizenship through naturalisation, this is not necessarily permanent. Naturalised citizenship may also be revoked: though numbers of citizenship revocations are small, a range of Western countries have recently introduced legislation to permit this. The case of Shamima Begum, a 15-year-old schoolgirl who travelled from the UK to Syria to support Islamic State, shows the consequences. Begum's UK citizenship was revoked because of national security concerns. The UK Supreme Court said this was lawful because she was also a Bangladeshi citizen and thus would not be made stateless, even though Bangladesh disagreed. As a result, Begum – who was born and grew up in England – can no longer claim citizenship of the country she was once a citizen of.

Citizenship, then, is a political question rather than a 'natural right'. This section focuses on citizenship debates in two contexts, Denmark and India, to examine the national social geographies of precarity. These geographies have direct consequences on people's lives where some persons are guaranteed the rights and privileges of citizenship while others are not based on social differences.

CITIZENSHIP AND BELONGING IN DENMARK

Denmark is one of several European countries that has made it more difficult for people to become citizens. It takes on average around 16 years to obtain Danish citizenship, and around a third of young people who were born and raised in Denmark are not Danish citizens. Denmark, as a Nordic country, has a reputation for being a liberal democracy, but its citizenship requirements are described as "some of the toughest in the world".[5] These requirements are particularly directed towards making it more difficult for Muslims to become naturalised Danish citizens. At the same time, Denmark is also removing status from (mostly Muslim) Syrian refugees, by saying that refugee status is temporary rather than permanent. A refugee is someone who has a well-founded fear of persecution that makes it impossible for them to return to their home country. A person who is accepted to be a refugee is generally treated like a citizen of a country, and refugee status has traditionally been seen as permanent. The Danish state is no longer recognising refugee status for certain minorities as permanent and, in the case of some Syrians, is revoking their rights to stay in Denmark and seeking to return them to Syria.[6] This action results in precarity for many migrants living in Denmark, because they have no guarantee of a future life in that country.

Citizenship requirements also give important insights into how states frame their relationship with ethnic/racial minority or migrant residents. The increasingly restrictive Danish naturalisation and refugee rules are mirrored in how the state approaches Muslims who live in the country. In early 2018, the Danish government proposed banning full face coverings in public places. The justice minister at that time, Søren Pape Poulsen, said, "It is incompatible with the values in Danish society and disrespectful to the community to keep one's face hidden when meeting each other in public spaces".[7] This became law in the middle of the same year, despite opposition (Figure 3.1). Denmark is one of an increasing number of European countries and regions, for example, Belgium, Bulgaria, France, Netherlands, and parts of Switzerland, that have upheld a ban on full face coverings in public places.[8] The justice minister's statement helps us to understand the link between the banning of full face coverings and the values of liberal democratic societies in ways that create precarities concerning mobilities and safety.

Liberal democracies such as Denmark create public/private distinctions in social lives. This means that in public places, people need to present themselves in an unmarked way in order to fit into the norms of a place that is supposedly devoid of distinguishing marks of ethnicity and religion. These norms can also inform

Figure 3.1 Protest against Niqab/Burqa Ban in Copenhagen, Denmark, 2018.

Source: Klaus Berdiin Jensen (www.flickr.com/photos/134331036@N08/43789623261/in/photostream/).

how in certain places people, particularly women, are expected to present themselves as accessible, allowing easy communication, dialogue, and interaction in the public sphere. A face covering is thought to come in the way of such dialogic communication in the public sphere. In liberal democracies, not showing your face can be seen as 'oppressive', marking the body not only in terms of religion and ethnicity but also as a specific form of gendered embodiment. Markers of ethnicity and religion are not entirely banned but some are relegated to the private sphere, such as to the home. A citizen's duty in these forms of liberal democracy is therefore to behave in a manner that respects the public/private distinction. This is thought to be the path to citizenship and belonging (Box 3.7). But how is this connected to precarity and liveability? The edict to stop wearing face covering means that women, in particular, are asked to compromise their religious adherence and cultural sensibilities. It also makes women wearing a *niqab* or a *hijab* vulnerable to attack and abuse in public places. Liberal democracies, while citing full face covering as an obstacle to communication in the public sphere, are also restricting the public sphere. In places like Denmark then you can only belong if you strip yourself of all ethnic and religious markers. The ban on full face coverings ends up targeting mostly

Muslim women and this is dangerous, given that they are already stereotyped as having no freedom by global Islamophobic forces.

BOX 3.7 CITIZENSHIP AND BELONGING

Geographers often understand citizenship as a form of belonging. In the case of citizenship, what does it mean to belong to a nation or a state? For instance, if a US citizen is entering the United States, immigration officials will often say 'welcome home'. As geographers, we need to ask, who gets to hear this statement and who does not? Does everyone who has a US passport or a permanent resident card get to hear this, or only some? An exact answer to these questions is not possible, as it usually depends on the skin colour and names of the people on both sides of the immigration counter, and the location of the port of entry. Stereotypes and assumptions that emerge from a social group's history in that country or in the world also mediate such interactions. From this, we see that belonging, when considered with citizenship, may often be hierarchical, tied to histories of difference and oppression, which make people precarious.

HIERARCHIES OF BELONGING IN INDIA

Citizenship both reflects and shapes social geographies of difference. This can be seen in the hierarchies of citizenship and belonging that are developing in India. These hierarchies create precarity, particularly for Muslims. A tripartite set of citizenship laws, starting in 2010, has led to this precarity. First, the National Population Register (NPR) was introduced in 2010. The NPR is a register of people living in an area for at least six months. Second, the National Register of Citizens (NRC) was initially introduced in Assam, a state in the north-east of India, in 2013 and is due to be implemented nationwide. The NRC is a register of all legal citizens of India, and it is based on the NPR. The purpose of the NRC is to identify and deport undocumented immigrants, particularly those who are Muslim. The third is the Citizenship Amendment Act (CAA), which was passed in 2019. The CAA offers a route to Indian citizenship for religious minority refugees – Buddhist, Christian, Hindu, Jain, Parsi, and Sikh – from the neighbouring countries of Afghanistan,

Bangladesh, and Pakistan. Remarkably and deliberately, there is no mention of Muslim refugees in this list.

In 2018–2019, India saw waves of protests against the tripartite laws (Figure 3.2). Critics argue that the laws specifically target Muslims and can lead to precarity for those who are economically marginalised with little or no access to work opportunities, health care, and education. In an early exercise on the NRC in Assam, more than one million persons were left out of the register, some of whom had been living in the region for generations. Being left off the register has severe consequences. For many who have not been officially recognised as Indian citizens, it means that they are effectively stateless, subject to detention and/or deportation, unless they can prove their citizenship through so-called 'Foreigners Tribunals'. People who are not included on the NRC are legally precarious, and many live in fear.

The counting in Assam also has had intersectional effects with immediate impact felt by transgender people. This is because it is impossible for most transgender persons to prove their lineage. Many trans persons are alienated from their families due to prejudice against their gendered lives, and many have genders, names, and religions that are different from those assigned in their birth certificates, resulting in

Figure 3.2 Protests against New Citizenship Laws in Shaheen Bagh, New Delhi, Led by Muslim Women.

Source: DiplomatTesterMan, Wikimedia Commons. https://commons.wikimedia.org/w/index.php?curid=85617824

This file is licensed under the Creative Commons Attribution-Share Alike 4.0 International license (https://creativecommons.org/licenses/by-sa/4.0/deed.en).

discrepancies in documented proof of citizenship. The discriminatory effects of the citizenship laws are already a reality for about 2000 transgender people who have been excluded from the NRC in Assam.[9]

The combined exclusionary logic of the NPR, NRC, and CAA is pushing Muslims and other minority and/or marginalised groups, such as Dalits, Adivasis, the landless, transgender, and queer persons, into terrains of further precarity by oppressive regimes. The three laws together have the power to render these groups, who are already marginalised in a patriarchal, caste-based society, stateless. This has potentially severe consequences. If a person is unable to show land and tenancy documents, birth certificates, bank account documents, educational certificates, and so on to prove their citizenship according to the NRC's definitions, they could be sent to detention camps already nearing completion in many parts of India. There is, however, a catch here. If a person is unable to prove their citizenship and therefore is not included in the NRC, they could, ideally, appeal to gain back their citizenship through the CAA. However, this is only if they are Hindu, Sikh, Jain, Christian, Buddhist, or Parsi. If they are Muslim, they are not only rendered stateless by the NRC but also banned from redressing the issue through the CAA. This means that they are rendered an illegal immigrant. In addition, for many transgender people whose names ended up appearing in Assam's NRC, the exercise was futile – as the list contained their birth-assigned or dead name and gender.

As the examples of Denmark and India illustrate, access to citizenship is a political decision that helps to form geographies of precarity at the national scale, with consequences at other scales and for people's lived experience. This is one of the ways in which precarity is created. In the next section, we highlight how economic structures also serve to create precarity.

III. PRECARIOUS SPACES: GLOBALISATION OF CORPORATIONS, DIGITAL LABOUR, AND GIG ECONOMIES

Economic structures create and sustain geographies of precarity at a range of scales, from the global to the intimate. Early research by geographers focused on precarious work but expanded to recognise how broader economic structures – such as globalisation and neoliberalism – created the conditions that allowed precarious work to proliferate. In this section, we will first focus on these economic structures in a discussion of the globalisation of corporations. We then shift our attention to the scale of the individual and the workplace, with a discussion of digital labour and gig economies. Our aim in this section is to highlight the relationship between economy and precarity, in ways that affect people across the world.

For many of us, engagement with paid employment is necessary for our survival (Box 3.8). We work to earn income, and that income in turn sustains us: it is how we pay for housing and food and other basic necessities for survival. If paid employment is insecure – whether this relates to poor pay, dangerous conditions, or work that is not recognised as employment – this creates precarity that can lead to injury or, in some cases, death. Thus, how labour is organised creates different forms of precarity, where some lives are valued more than others. This varies geographically including through national legislations that protect work (think of the health and safety laws and how these can be ignored and/or undermined), transnational corporate policies, and workplace practices. Our security and survival, in many instances, depends on our ability to engage with the economy through paid employment, but the conditions of employment may result in precarity.

BOX 3.8 LABOUR AND PAID EMPLOYMENT

Labour is the undertaking of work, including both paid employment and work that is unpaid. Paid employment can dominate discussions of labour and the focus of social geographers is on the inequitable distribution of resources particularly in capitalist and neoliberal systems. These systems work to create profit by extracting labour at a cheaper price than the goods/services produced are sold for. Labour creates different forms of precariousness for social groups. This varies locally (think of managers compared to workers), regionally (consider 'head office' compared to regional spaces), nationally (consider the different labour laws, who has the right to create or join unions to support them, health and safety regulations), and internationally (how billionaires that own and run companies maximise profits by creating precarity for their workers).

Welfare states may provide for those who are not employed, for example through housing support, food support, and unemployment benefits. However, welfare supports from the state are heavily regulated, with conditions on who can access them, and for how long. Media, political, and public opinion can often be critical of those in receipt of welfare supports. Under neoliberal regimes in particular, poverty is often individualised and associated with laziness, with the result that welfare recipients may be represented as the 'undeserving poor'. This can relate to class, race, gender, and disability, as well as migration and citizenship status. Often the protection of 'our own' can be used to contest provision to refugees and other migrants, without the associated support for those who are 'our own' who are equally considered 'undeserving'. This has intensified under neoliberalism and globalisation. Now, a significant proportion of people are categorised as 'working poor'. Though they have paid employment, their rate of pay is so low that they are at risk of poverty. Neoliberalism, globalisation, and changing work practices have all contributed to this intensified precarity, and we discuss these in turn.

GLOBALISATION OF CORPORATIONS: IRELAND'S TAX STATUS

Under globalisation, companies and businesses have developed through transnational networks and connections. These have enabled the pursuit of profit through neoliberal capitalist hegemonies across the globe (Box 3.9). One way that companies exploit neoliberal regimes is to source low-paid labour in places that are less subject to safety/health/employment restrictions, and to use these low-paid workers to create goods that are then sold for high prices in other places around the world as part of global commodity chains that we discussed in terms of clothes in Chapter 2. Usually this can be considered in terms of low-wage employment in the Global South and lucrative markets in the Global North, but this is too simplistic. For example, in the US, prisoners can be used as low-wage workers to produce goods/parts cheaply that are distributed globally. Similarly, there are lucrative markets in the Global South where luxury commodities are distributed (for example, the sale of Scottish whisky to China). Nonetheless, the globalisation of corporations connects different parts of the world in ways that reproduce geopolitical differences through the effects it has on people's everyday lives, making some lives more precarious than others.

BOX 3.9 NEOLIBERALISM

Neoliberalism is an economic ideology that is currently dominant globally. It advocates for limitations/reductions in state policies and regulations. This is based on the belief that limited state policies and regulations encourage an economic free market that, in turn, will lead to increased profits and socio-economic improvements. However, this idea of the social good of neoliberalism has been shown to be inaccurate. Instead, neoliberalism creates precarity and further social inequality.

While companies can move around the globe, they have often been subject to restrictions and regulations. The globalisation of companies or corporations rests on the marketisation of places and neoliberal policies that remove or reduce restrictions and regulations. For instance, in order to sell goods in the European Union, companies need to have a base there or pay a 'Common Customs Tariff'. This varies depending on the type of goods being imported and where they are coming from. Since the 1990s, Ireland – a member of the EU – has sought to attract companies from outside the EU (often from the US). A base in Ireland allows international companies to sell goods across the EU without paying a tariff. However, Ireland wanted to attract international companies in order to promote employment, and it did this by offering low corporate taxation rates on profits. This was 12.5% at the time of writing, but the effective tax rate is closer to 2–2.5% for global profits moved into Ireland. In this way, Ireland markets itself to international companies, and has been particularly successful in attracting those in high-tech and pharmaceutical sectors. Ireland has become an advantageous place for international companies that want to access the EU market and/or avail of a low tax rate on profits. Ireland's tax regime and membership of the EU are key reasons why the country has moved from an impoverished nation post-independence from the United Kingdom in 1922 to one that is now economically wealthy. Between 1995 and 2007 Ireland was referred to as the 'Celtic Tiger', a reference to Asian (Tiger) economies that grew rapidly. This has had an effect on people's lives at a range of scales. For example, it has increased the amount and types of employment provided in Ireland – often in Dublin – and the tax revenue that the Irish state receives, making lives economically less vulnerable for some. At the same time, it has resulted in the loss of employment and tax revenue for other people and places in Ireland, creating other forms of precariousness.

Yet the case of Ireland also shows how global corporations and international organisations, in conjunction with national governments, implement local regimes of precarity. For example, neoliberal policies reduced regulation on borrowing and property prices and lending significantly increased. When the global housing market crash began in 2008, Ireland was badly affected. The amount of lending and lack of regulation meant there was a significant banking crash. An 85 billion euro bailout for Ireland from the European Union and the International Monetary Fund was directed towards ensuring that banks did not collapse. The bailout came with stringent austerity measures, including wage cuts and the privatisation of state services. This meant that those who were most affected by the bailout were those on lower and middle incomes, state employees, those who were unemployed, and those reliant on state benefits, rather than those who had caused the financial crisis. Despite the financial difficulties Ireland faced, there was no attempt to increase corporation tax rates. Instead, when the European Commission ruled that Apple needed to pay 13 billion euro plus interest to the Irish state – the European Commission said this was unpaid tax from 2004 to 2014 – the Irish government rejected the payment and appealed the ruling. There was some resistance to austerity measures, most notably in relation to efforts to introduce water charges for domestic households. As a private company attempted to install water meters, groups of local residents began to block them, concerned that this was the first step in the privatisation of water supplies. The protests spread nationwide, with the result that domestic water charges have not been introduced, demonstrating resistance and resilience in the face of powerful government and international institutions.

At the time of writing in 2023, within Ireland there are significant disparities and precarities related to global corporations and their tax operations, as well as the neoliberal regimes that led to the banking crisis. There is a two-tier healthcare system in Ireland, with public health systems under significant pressure. Long public waiting lists limit access to timely healthcare for those who rely on the public system. In contrast, people who can afford to pay privately for healthcare – whether directly or through private health insurance – receive rapid treatment, often in public hospitals. Access to housing is an increasing problem. Successive neoliberal Irish governments have not invested in public housing, so people increasingly rely on the private housing market. The cost of housing has been rising, in part through the purchase of housing for profit by global corporations either through rental incomes or through property values. Houses built during the Celtic Tiger era and beyond have been shown to have significant structural flaws, as builders self-certify their work. This has direct implications for the availability of safe homes. The tax regime within the country is criticised and challenged by those who want to see better redistribution of wealth. They see that higher taxation could be used to improve housing, healthcare, and offer other societal benefits. The taxation scheme has also come under pressure internationally, as in 2021 a global deal set the minimum tax rate for large corporations at 15%. Ireland was one of the last countries to agree to this deal, after it won concessions to prevent a higher rate of tax.

Ireland shows how companies can move easily from place to place to take advantage of favourable conditions. These movements have effects on the wealth of a country and its ability to provide for its citizens and residents. While in some cases global corporations move to pay employees less and, in this way, increase profits, in the case of Ireland, tax regimes and access to the EU market create favourable conditions to increase companies' profits. These global corporations impact lives in Ireland by providing employment, including in highly skilled, high-paid jobs, but this does not address areas of low pay or precarity. We will now turn to explore the gig economy and the use of digital platforms by global corporations in ways that create precarity through informal labour markets.

DIGITAL LABOUR AND GIG ECONOMIES

We now live in a digital world. Digital technology has changed how societies and economies work, and this transformation has been intensified by COVID-19, as people in lockdown looked for new ways to engage in necessary and desired social and economic activities. Think about all the ways in which our everyday lives are now shaped by digital technology. Many of us bank and shop online. We use our phones to find our way, watch films, or listen to music streamed by cloud computing services. We connect with friends and perform our identities online, using apps that allow us to share images, sound, and videos. Perhaps we now work from home, using high-speed internet to connect us to colleagues and information. We rely on digital technology extensively, which in turn gives rise to new kinds of economic activities (Box 3.10).

> ## BOX 3.10 DIGITAL ECONOMY
>
> The digital economy refers to economic activities that use computing and codes with algorithms. Research on the digital economy is particularly concerned with how digital technology transforms economic activities such as production and consumption.

Digital technology has had a particular impact on work. The term 'digital labour' is often used to describe how work has been affected by technology (Box 3.11). However, a lot of work is now directly or indirectly affected by computing and codes with algorithms – for example, using word processing, mobile phones or GPS, using cloud computing, working on assembly lines, or in agriculture that uses digital technology to optimise activities. Given the broad scope of the work, an equally broad definition is not particularly helpful. Instead, we use digital labour in a more focused way.

> ## BOX 3.11 DIGITAL LABOUR
>
> This term was first used to describe unpaid work on social media platforms (for example, 'likes' on Facebook) that was used to extract value. As technology has changed, the term has also changed in meaning. A recent definition suggested that digital labour is the work of users and formal employees in digital media industries, as well as work that is mediated by digital platforms.[10]

We are particularly interested in how digital labour results in precarity. Remember our definition of precarity: people who are more prone to injury because of what is happening in their socio-structural context. We want to show how the development of digital platforms (Box 3.12) is one of these socio-structural changes that results in precarity in people's work lives, and their lives in general.

BOX 3.12 DIGITAL PLATFORM

This is an internet site or app that connects users (workers) and potential employers. Common examples include transport services such as Uber; delivery services such as Deliveroo and Zomato; and personal service provision platforms such as Handy and Care App.

Often, digital platforms are connected to gig economies (Box 3.13). The gig economy uses technology to create precarious (freelance) workers who can be connected to customers via a digital platform. The platform takes a percentage of the money earned and workers are not employed by those who run the digital platform.

BOX 3.13 GIG ECONOMY

A gig economy relies on temporary or part-time workers, who are generally freelance rather than employees. It's easy to understand when we think about music gigs: musicians are hired to perform for a short time at events, like a party or wedding, rather than being employed by the event venue.

A gig economy is profitable for employers: they don't have to pay the worker other than when a service is needed; they don't have to pay social insurance contributions or make payments for holidays or sick leave. Some workers like the flexibility of gig economy employment, and the fact that they can charge more for their short-term work; but many workers have no option but to work in this way, and they have no security of employment. Therefore, workers are always temporary without any job security or benefits.

This is being contested through digital unionisation where workers develop unions via social media and other technologies to work together to resist exploitation (Figure 3.3).

Digital platforms enable gig economies, particularly because digital platforms often insist that workers who use their services are independent contractors rather than employees. For example, Uber recruitment material emphasises the potential for independence: some of the phrases used on their website include 'Make money when you want', 'Set your own schedule', and 'Make money on your terms'.[11] The independence and freedom promised are mostly illusory. Research on the experiences of Uber drivers in Washington DC concluded that "the economic realities of precarious work are a far cry from the rosy promises of the gig economy".[12] Uber drivers in that city were described as being on a "debt-to-work pipeline", taking on debt to buy or lease a car and maintain it, with no guarantee of work or income, and no ability to influence how the company operates. In Brazil, food delivery drivers reported longer working hours and less pay during the pandemic.[13] These

Figure 3.3 Gig Economy Strikers in Italy.

Source: "fighting for rights in the gig economy" by Davide Alberani (www.flickr.com/photos/29150263@N07/32290856168) licensed under CC BY-SA 2.0 (https://creativecommons.org/licenses/by-sa/2.0/).

stories are repeated across the 17 different countries investigated by Fairwork, an organisation concerned with working conditions in the platform economy. In Egypt, for example, Fairwork found that gig workers face a wide range of risks and rarely receive fair pay. In Ghana, while gig workers often received the minimum wage, this was at a very low rate, and workers did not have access to fair contracts.[14] In order to make even more profits, digital platforms seek to minimise costs by pushing as much as possible onto workers. Gig economies and digital platforms – sometimes called platform economies – lead to precarity in place for workers who, without any security of employment, struggle to make a decent living. This type of gig work is most often available in cities, where time-poor residents seek to outsource the work of social reproduction – like food preparation – but want access quickly and cheaply.

Digital platforms also enable another form of work, which is variously called remote work or outsourcing or cloudwork. Rather than the gig economy being local, some people now say it is global or planetary. Labour markets no longer need to be proximate: instead, workers and employers can learn about each other and jobs using digital technology. This contrasts with the use of face-to-face meetings and job vacancies advertised in local print media or by word of mouth. One of the sectors that has made considerable use of cloudworkers is publishing. Much of the work of publishers, such as copyediting and proofreading, and producing page proofs, can be done digitally and remotely, and so publishing companies have been reducing staff numbers globally, and contracting freelancers instead. You should check to see if this cloudwork is visible in any of the textbooks you use during your studies. The growth of this 'planetary labour market', enabled by digital platforms, is leading to precarity for workers in several ways. There is an oversupply of workers, often from lower-income countries; these workers are often competitors rather than collaborators; and they are usually not protected by labour laws.[15] Because of this, cloudworkers may also experience precarity, similar to the gig workers who experience precarity in place.

However, just as digital technology is used to benefit employers and corporations at the expense of workers, there are also efforts by workers to use digital technology, as well as other means, to improve their work conditions. In a variety of different contexts, gig workers use messaging platforms, such as WhatsApp and Facebook, to share experiences, build solidarity, and to collectively organise. Acts of resistance include small-scale and localised protests over working conditions, everyday forms of resistance such as deliberate delays, and more structured mobilisation, such as the legal case taken by Uber drivers in London, leading to them being recognised as workers by the UK Supreme Court.[16]

On balance, though, digital platforms and gig economies have changed the nature of work so that it is now, across the world, more insecure. Costs and risks are passed on to workers – for example, the cost of equipment, the risk of illness – so that the worker needs to invest money before getting work and will only get paid for the hours he/she works. There is often little or no regulation of gig work, so workers are not adequately paid or protected. With no limits on entry into gig work, increased competition means less pay, with workers having to work for longer and unsafe hours to survive. Rather than the promised freedom and flexibility, gig workers experience precarity because of the changing socio-structural context that fails to treat them as workers, that fails to hold their employers responsible for ensuring decent work; and that places workers in competition with each other locally and globally. Gig work is the opposite of decent work, one of the UN's Sustainable Development Goals.[17]

IV. LIVEABLE LIVES: THE POSSIBILITIES OF LIVING

While the concept of liveable lives speaks to precarity and the ways in which difference affects bodies, it also enables hope. This could be hope for a life that is more liveable, a 'good life' (Box 3.14), or a politics of liveability that strives for more. How do marginalised communities imagine and work towards liveable lives by facing and critiquing their precarity? How do they dream and build (im)possible futures? What does this life look like against the larger grammar of place that translates into violence for oppressed communities every time they reimagine and contest power? This section showcases the power of the collective in seeking and ushering changes to the precarity of lives that marginalised communities face. We will first look at how Pride and the related moments of celebration/advocacy offer glimpses into the possibilities of the 'good life' for some. We will then, through the example of a dairy farm in India, look at how the geographies of precarity become spaces of resilience and social change.

> ## BOX 3.14 GOOD LIFE
>
> Butler speaks not only about survival but also about a good life that goes beyond survival and a bare life. She argues that "One can survive without being able to live one's life. And in some cases, it surely does not seem worth it to survive under such conditions. So, an overarching demand must be precisely for a liveable life – that is, a life that can be lived".[18] A life that can be lived may be achievable or it may be a utopian goal depending on the precarity of your life. This politics does more than ask for the bare minimum for survival and instead seeks a recognition that all lives should be made liveable.

PRIDE

Lesbian, gay, bisexual, trans, queer, intersex people, and those who have identities, lives, desires, relationships, and genders outside of what is considered 'normal' (LGBTQI+) are often subject to pressure to live in particular ways. This can vary from state laws that forbid and punish same-sex acts, to hostile media stories, to everyday street harassment. LGBTQI+ people are often precarious because of the ways in which sexuality and gender are 'supposed' to be, perhaps linked to religious doctrine or to assumptions about what is 'natural'. Under these conditions, it can be difficult to make lives survivable.

Yet across time and place, LGBTQI+ people and communities have defied the rules of sexualities and genders in home spaces and at public events. Pride events can allow people to gather, to celebrate, and to protest in ways that are not possible at other points in the year. Pride events create specific forms of space. Participants usually march through places that have meaning where they are, such as a town centre (that is usually heterosexual), a particular site where an attack has occurred, or places where, in other circumstances, LGBTQI+ people would feel different. They (temporarily) transform the spaces where the march takes place. What is usually straight space becomes comfortable for same-sex and same-gender couples to hold hands and kiss. Some gender non-conformity is also on display and celebrated, though trans (and bi) people have also had some difficult experiences at Pride events. Pride brings people together around a shared identity or shared hope for change, while highlighting discrimination, violence, and abuse. Pride events have been important in transforming the position of LGBTQI+ people in some societies and celebrating their lives as valid, important and fun! Pride can make life more liveable for LGBTQI+ people as the resonances of the day last for longer than the day itself.

The annual Delhi Queer Pride gives us some insights into how lives become liveable even for a short time (Figure 3.4). It starts very close to what appears to be the heart of the city, Connaught Place, with an arch made of rainbow-coloured balloons, banners, and posters with slogans that question fascism, Islamophobia, and homo-nationalisms, ask for anti-caste rights, advocate for gay marriage, or simply state 'love is love'. Thousands of people, young and old, across the social spectrum of caste, class, religion, genders, and sexualities, march for a stretch of roughly three kilometres. As with

Figure 3.4 The Start-point of Delhi Pride (Map showing the small public toilet transformed into a dressing room); Background image of Pride banner of Delhi Queer Pride (modified).

Sources: Map from Google Earth. Background Pride image by Ramesh Lalwani, https://commons.wikimedia.org/wiki/File:Delhi_Queer_Pride_parade.jpg–CCBY2.0(https://creativecommons.org/licenses/by/2.0).

116   GEOGRAPHIES OF PRECARITY

a lot of Pride events, this is possible because of police/state permissions. The first Pride in Delhi happened in 2008. When activists approached the authorities to request permission for the march, they struggled to explain what identities, bodies, and rights it represented. The rubric of queerness was new and difficult, a Western concept, and thus alien to the authorities. So, the activists sought permission for a march in the name of women's rights, a political and social project that had gained tremendous currency through a strong feminist movement, and through NGOs and transnational funding. The first Pride event in Delhi was small, and people wore masks to protect their identities and livelihoods. Now, thousands of people walk in Pride, many without masks, and similar Pride events also take place in several small towns in India. This is in line with the global presence of such events through a politics of visibility; media report Pride as a gala event with pictures of Hijras and Kothis dancing and/or non-heterosexual couples kissing in public view.

There are various liveabilities created through the march and the reclaiming of space. We will point to two. Next to where Pride starts and thousands gather to paint the city rainbow, there is a small public toilet. It is an ordinary run-down toilet but a closer glimpse inside, right before the Pride event begins, presents a different picture. Many participants come from home already dressed in glitter and fabulous attire. However, some leave their homes wearing normative clothes that conform to their assigned gender. Inside the toilet, these normative clothes are gradually undone, as the place is transformed into a dressing room by some participants in Pride. One helps another wear a saree, while someone is applying makeup and eyeliner on the other. This toilet becomes a transformative space that allows queerness to survive. At the other end of this march is Jantar Mantar, a historical site and scientific observatory that was built in the eighteenth century. It is next to the area designated by the state for holding almost all the protests in the national capital. Here a contained geography of protests and resistances is produced by the state for easy control, barricaded by police and the presence of water cannons, and close to Parliament Street police station. Any protest elsewhere in the city's landscape, especially outside embassies and state buildings, results in police crackdown and brutalities, water cannons, lathi charges, and detentions. The procession of dancing queers culminates here and joins with other protests. While

GEOGRAPHIES OF PRECARITY   **117**

the queers stake claims to become the citizen–subject addressing the law and social moralities of their geographies, they share this space with other protestors. This could be a Dalit mother seeking justice for the institutional murder of her son in the Hyderabad central university who has joined a Muslim mother whose son went missing from a prominent university in the capital after a feud with the student wing of the ruling party. Or it could also be a group of farmers from Tamil Nadu in the south of India, who have travelled thousands of miles to plead for loan waivers from the central government amidst growing number of farmer suicides. Many of them have shaved half their moustaches and heads, and they gesture to their plight by holding the skulls of dead farmers in their hands. Next to it could be a procession of Muslim men seeking justice for 16-year-old Junaid who was stabbed to death in a hate crime on the Delhi–Mathura train while returning from Eid shopping. This juxtaposition gives this place a curious character. It is telling of the precarities of a diverse set of people, speaking to the seat of power in different voices and ways. From the public toilet at the beginning of Pride to this ensemble of protests at the end of it, there is hope, there is anger, there is frustration and yet resilience.

While Pride allows some LGBTQI+ people to experience a good life, if even for a few hours, it is not enough. Protests, contestations, and actions are key for some to create lives as liveable. Pride events started as protests that were explicitly political in seeking equalities, rights and changes to heterosexual/gender normative cultures. Pride also has been increasingly commercialised, particularly in the Global North, with access to Pride influenced by money as well as 'acceptability' in ways that create and reflect differences between LGBTQI+ people. Increasingly 'the party' has become more and more prominent in ways that suggest Pride is no longer political. Of course, each city has its own version of Pride, and there is no one 'Pride' event. As we have seen with the case of New Delhi, the party can be empowering, enabling a break from, if not an end to, precarious lives. Making life liveable by being able to dress, act, and dance is powerful, but Pride is not ordinary. Its power lies in its extraordinary status, such that the liveabilities that it creates are fleeting. Moreover, it only creates liveabilities for some. For others unable to access the event or experiencing racial, class, able-bodied, gendered, age, and other forms of prejudice, Pride can make life less liveable.

TRANS ACTIVISM IN INDIA: GRACE BANU AND THE MILK CO-OPERATIVE SOCIETY

It is estimated that around 2 million people in India are trans. Trans people, particularly Hijras, have been vilified for decades, particularly following the colonial-era Criminal Tribes Act of 1871. Due to social ostracisation, lack of support systems, and limited opportunities, most trans people are either engaged in *badhai* (community practices of blessing the newlyweds and newborns by Hijras), begging at traffic lights and in public transport, and sex work.

In a landmark judgment in 2014, the Supreme Court of India recognised transgenders as citizen subjects underlining their historical marginalisation and ostracisation. The judgment began with acknowledging that "seldom our society realizes or cares to realize the trauma, pain, and agony which members of the Transgender community undergo". The judgment lays down important measures to address the discriminatory practices, such as affirmative action in education and employment.[19] Unfortunately, the government of India passed the Transgender Persons (Protection of Rights) Act in 2019, which undermines both the Supreme Court judgment and demands from the trans community despite the latter's persistent resistance. This Act has solidified transphobia through gender screening tests, differential treatment in terms of sexual harassment through a lower penalty compared to women, and no guarantee of reserved positions in education or employment. Despite the legal recognition of the 2014 judgment, trans people continue to face considerable challenges, exacerbated by the 2019 Act.

The transgender community in India is not a homogenous identity. Social fissures such as caste and class percolate within the community and create further hierarchies of existence. Several trans activists in India, such as Grace Banu, Living Smile Vidya, and Nutan, have highlighted caste biases within the community through their writings and activisms. Of the many stories of resilience in India that trans persons personify through their everyday practices, we intend to highlight one. Grace Banu is a Dalit trans woman from the state of Tamil Nadu in Southern part of India. A formidable voice in trans rights activism in the country, she is the first trans woman to be trained as a software engineer. Growing up, she faced challenges of caste-based untouchability and transphobia and yet her resilient spirit has paved the way in bringing tremendous change for not only herself but many other trans persons. Banu has spearheaded a Dalit Bahujan[20] centred organisation that works with trans persons. She has sought to gain recognition for trans people to appear in Public Service examinations conducted by her home state, Tamil Nadu, and to obtain ration cards for trans persons during COVID-19 to assure they can avail state aid and support. She has equally been vociferous in fighting against the Vedanta Corporation's Sterlite copper smelting plant in Thoothukudi which would contaminate local water bodies and bring into precarity the sole source of livelihood of the local fishing community. Banu has also been petitioning in courts for horizontal reservations for the trans community. Horizontal reservation is one of two forms of affirmative action in India: the other is vertical reservation, which provides for affirmative action for specific castes such as Scheduled Castes, Scheduled Tribes, and Other Backwards Classes. The introduction of horizontal reservations would ensure reservations for trans people in every vertical category of caste. For example, if the horizontal quota for trans people is 2%, then 2% of the reservations in every caste category, for example Scheduled Castes, must also be 2%. Horizontal reservations would acknowledge the intersectional ways in which transphobia and casteism operate in Indian society, and would ensure that trans people would not be forced into choosing one social identity over another.

One of the ways in which Grace Banu has helped to create liveable lives is through the establishment of the Milk Co-operative Society in Thoothukudi in July 2019.[21] After seven years of persistent struggle, Banu and other trans women activists were able to open India's first trans women–run dairy farm and registered milk co-operative society, located three kilometres from Kovilpatti village. The farm and its associated housing is called Sandeep Nagar, and it is named after the district collector Sandeep Nanduri who helped set it up. Sandeep Nagar hosts 85 trans women under the government's residential and livelihood scheme. Rather than isolating this dairy farm at the periphery of the settlement – where Dalit and trans communities are usually forced to locate – Grace Banu made sure the settlement of trans women redefining their lives in the course of dignity and equality is part of the social imagination of the place. Trans lives are often reduced to discrimination and death, recounted on the trans day of remembrance. In contrast,

Grace Banu and her fellow activists are imagining new worlds of hope that challenge precarities of caste, class, gender, and sexualities (Figure 3.5).

V. CONCLUSION

In this chapter, we discuss the geographies of precarity. We introduce you to the concepts of precariousness and precarity. We demonstrate the importance of geography for understanding precarity, because lives are made to be less secure in ways that differ across place and space. Using a range of case studies, we illustrate the geographies of precarity across different scales. We begin by discussing citizenship. With examples from Denmark and India, we show how access to citizenship may lead to precarity for those whose access is restricted, denied, or removed. We next discuss the relationship between broader economic structures – such as globalisation and employment – and precarity. Our case studies focus on the precarious spaces that are enabled by neoliberalism, the globalisation of corporations, and the growth of digital labour and gig economies. We then highlight ways in which different groups and individuals have challenged precarity in an effort to construct liveable lives, with a discussion of Pride and trans activism.

The geographies of precarity and liveability allow us to discuss and consider the politics of living. If all humans are precarious, precarity shows us that we are closer/farther away from being able

Figure 3.5 Sandeep Nagar Dairy Farm, Managed and Run by Trans Women in Tamil Nadu, India.

Source: Grace Banu.

to live because of things like our citizenship, employment prospects, laws and communities. However, a chapter that focuses only on precarity is not consistent with the message of our book. It is equally important that we highlight liveability as a counter to precarity. For this reason, the chapter also explores the creation of liveable lives and good lives as political aims: whether temporary or longer-lasting, whether local or translocal. This is important because it allows us to hope by acknowledging how people organise, resist, and thrive, even as we seek to contest the inequitable geographies that create their lives.

NOTES

1 Butler, J. (2010) *Frames of War: When Is Life Grievable?* London: Verso, p. 25.
2 Butler, J. (2012) "Can one lead a good life in a bad life?". *Radical Philosophy* 176: 9–18. Available online at www.radicalphilosophy.com/article/can-one-lead-a-good-life-in-a-bad-life.
3 Mbembe, A. (2019) *Necropolitics* (trans. S. Corcoran). Durham and London: Duke University Press, p. 37.
4 Mbembe, A. (2003) "Necropolitics". *Public Culture* 15(1): 11–40, p. 16. https://doi.org/10.1215/08992363-15-1-11.
5 European Commission (2021) *Denmark Tightens Rules for Citizenship Once Again.* Available online at https://ec.europa.eu/migrant-integration/news/denmark-tightens-rules-citizenship-once-again_en [accessed 16 April 2022].
6 Jacobsen, M. H. (2021) *Making and Breaking Families in Danish Nation-Building.* Available online at thedisorderofthings.com/2021/05/20/making-and-breaking-families-in-danish-nation-building/ [accessed 16 April 2022].
7 Agence France-Press (2018) "Danish government proposes ban on full-face veils". *Guardian*, 6 February. Available online at www.theguardian.com/world/2018/feb/06/danish-government-proposes-ban-on-full-face-veils [accessed 3 January 2023].
8 Al Jazeera (2018) *Denmark Passes Law Banning Face Veil in Public Spaces.* Available online at www.aljazeera.com/news/2018/5/31/denmark-passes-law-banning-face-veil-in-public-spaces [accessed 3 January 2023].
9 Das, G. (2019) "The NRC poses a two-fold predicament for Assam's transgender community". *The Wire.* Available online at https://thewire.in/rights/nrc-exclusions-assam-transgender [accessed 27 February 2023].
10 Jarrett, K. (2022) *Digital Labor.* Cambridge and Medford, MA: Policy Press.
11 Uber (2022) *Opportunity Is Everywhere.* Available online at www.uber.com/ie/en/drive/ [accessed 21 June 2022].

12 Wells, K., D. Cullen and K. Attoh (2017) *The Work Lives of Uber Drivers: Worse than You Think*. Available online at www.lawcha.org/2017/08/08/work-lives-uber-drivers-worse-think/ [Accessed 21 June 2022].

13 Grohmann, R., R. Carelli, D. Abs, J. Salvagni, K. Howson, F. Ustek-Spilda and M. Graham (2020) *The Uprising of Brazilian Food Delivery Riders*. Available online at https://fair.work/en/fw/blog/the-uprising-of-brazilian-food-delivery-riders/ [Accessed 21 June 2022].

14 Fairwork (2022) *Ratings*. Available online at https://fair.work/en/fw/ratings/ [Accessed 21 June 2022].

15 Graham, M. and M. Amir Anwar (2019) "The global gig economy: Towards a planetary labour market?". *First Monday* 24(4). https://doi.org/10.5210/fm.v24i4.9913.

16 UK Supreme Court (2021) "Uber BV and others (Appellants) v Aslam and others (Respondents) [2021] UKSC 5 On appeal from: [2018] EWCA Civ 2748". *Press Summary*. Available online at www.supremecourt.uk/press-summary/uksc-2019-0029.html [accessed 16 April 2022].

17 For more information about the Sustainable Development Goals, see https://sdgs.un.org/goals.

18 Butler (2012), *op. cit.*, p. 15.

19 There is some confusion in how 'Transgender' is defined in the judgment, with both narrow biological essentialised definitions and broader definitions that include Hijras and other gender variant communities. See Dutta, A. (2014) "Contradictory tendencies: The Supreme Court's NALSA judgment on transgender recognition and rights". *Journal of Indian Law and Society* 5(Monsoon): 225–236.

20 Dalit Bahujan refers to 'untouchable' castes, Adivasis and subordinate caste-class groups. They form the majority of the Indian population but are socio-economically and politically dominated by Hindu middle and upper caste-class groups.

21 Archana, K. C. (28 October 2020). "Life of dignity: India's first state-backed Dairy Farm provides livelihood to transgenders". *India Times*. Retrieved February 23, 2023, from www.indiatimes.com/trending/human-interest/indias-first-trans-run-dairy-farm-526250.html.

FURTHER READING

BOOKS

Banerjea, N. and K. Browne (2023) *Liveable Lives*. London: Bloomsbury.

Butler, J. (2010) *Frames of War: When Is Life Grievable?* London: Verso.

Mbembe, A. (2019) *Necropolitics* (trans. S. Corcoran). Durham and London: Duke University Press.

Ness, I. (ed.) (2022) *The Routledge Handbook of the Gig Economy*. London and New York: Routledge.

JOURNALS

ACME: An International Journal for Critical Geographies. Available online at https://acme-journal.org/index.php/acme

Antipode: A Radical Journal of Geography. Available online at https://onlinelibrary.wiley.com/journal/14678330 and at https://antipodeonline.org/about-the-journal-and-foundation/a-radical-journal-of-geography/

JOURNAL ARTICLES

Antonsich, M. (2010) "Searching for belonging – An analytical framework." *Geography Compass*, 4(6), 644–659. https://doi.org/10.1111/j.1749-8198.2009.00317.x

Harris, E. and M. Nowicki (2018) "Cultural geographies of precarity." *Cultural Geographies*, 25(3), 387–391. https://doi.org/10.1177/1474474018762812

OTHER RESOURCES

Fairwork website and resources. Available online at https://fair.work/en/fw/homepage/

4

MOVEMENT, MIGRATION, MOBILITIES

I. INTRODUCTION

Human beings are mobile. They move several times during the day/night. They also move from one place to another; sometimes temporarily, sometimes for a longer period. Other living beings are also mobile, like birds, animals, and insects. In addition to the movement of people and fauna, our everyday lives also depend on many other forms of movement. For example, much of the food we eat is not produced locally, but is transported from other parts of the world. The same is true of the clothes we wear, and of the many other objects we need for everyday survival. Ideas about how we live or might live are also mobile, transported from one place to another in material form, such as by books or people, or virtually through technology. Movement and mobility is an important part of our lives; so important that we often overlook its presence.

Why do social geographers study movement? The main reason is that movement changes both places and social relations. Think about the places you know, and how they have been changed by movement. This might be new forms of transport – a cycle path, or a new road, or a new bus service. This could be the effects of tourism, like the new businesses that have developed or the influx of people at particular times of the year. Or perhaps you are familiar with a place that has been changed by migration? This could be a rural area that has lost young people who have moved away to study or work, or an urban area with a growing and diverse population. All of these types of movements affect social relations: sometimes positively; sometimes leading to tension and conflict. If you

DOI: 10.4324/9781003266877-5

reflect on the places you know, you will be able to identify different ways in which movement has changed them, and how people have responded to those changes.

BOX 4.1 MOBILITY AND IMMOBILITY

Mobility means movement from one place to another. There are lots of different ways in which people, animals, and things can move, including walking, running, cycling, driving, sailing, and flying. It's important to note that mobilities are not open to everyone. Immobility is the term used to indicate restrictions or bans on mobility. Difference plays a role in who and what can move and in what ways.

What types of movement do social geographers study? The most studied movement is migration, particularly the migration of people. Indeed, the roots of modern social geography lie in studying the impacts of migration on places, particularly cities. More recently, social geographers have also been interested in how migration creates new connections between places, connecting places and people across distances and international borders. Technology has made this easier, as people and places are connected through social media. Social geographers also study other forms of movement, such as the movement of things and ideas, and the changing ways in which people move. In recent years, this interest in other forms of movement has grown, influenced by the 'mobilities turn' in the social sciences. The mobilities turn looks at the interconnections of the movement of people, things, and ideas. It also examines the regimes and infrastructures that enable or restrict movement, and how these different and interconnected movements shape place and space. The mobilities turn insists that mobility is an ordinary and common part of everyday life, and that we need to study and understand mobility, and its consequences and exclusions, including immobility, in an integrated and holistic way (Box 4.1). For social geographers, this has two implications. The first is that we need to understand the relationship between movement and place broadly. The second is that we need to pay attention to how intersecting social locations and identities – for example, gender, race, class, caste, sexuality, religion, ethnicity, or nationality – influence, and are affected by, mobilities and movement.

Because of the mobilities turn, social geographers have also started to pay more attention to immobility – to the ways in which people or things or ideas are prevented from moving either by lack of accessible infrastructure or by national and international laws. Again, migration has been a key focus of these efforts (Box 4.2 and Box 4.3). In addition to studying the effects of migration, social geographers are interested in understanding who is prevented from migrating, and why. We ask questions about the broader global structures that make it difficult for people with certain nationalities, or living in particular places, to become international migrants. We think about the consequences of these limits and limitations, whether this is the growth in border walls around the world, or the migrants who become undocumented and live precarious lives as a result. Social geographers also pay attention to other forms of immobility, such as transport poverty, restrictions in the supply of goods or services, or the censorship of ideas. We ask, what are the consequences of immobility, or 'stuckness', for lives and locales? We have been forced to address this question directly since the emergence of COVID-19. During lockdowns, people around the world were required to remain in place as a means of restricting the spread of the disease. This enforced immobility occurred across a range of different scales, including local, national, and international. For example, localised lockdowns confined some people to their homes, and others to a small distance from where they lived. For Kath and Mary in Ireland, at times this meant they could only travel up to 2 km or 5 km from their homes. Often, within national borders, certain regions were put in lockdown to limit the spread of COVID-19, while other regions had fewer restrictions on mobility. Even when local and national restrictions were lifted, external borders often remained closed, so that people had to stay within their home country and were unable to travel internationally. For example, Australia closed its international borders to most people for almost two years, with a small number of exceptions for Australian citizens and residents. Lockdowns, which involved the imposition of immobility on residents, often had unintended mobility consequences. This was the case in India. Many internal migrants living in India's cities lost their livelihoods when their places of work were suddenly

Figure 4.1 Stranded Migrant Workers During a COVID-19 Lockdown in India.

Source: Sumita Roy Dutta, https://commons.wikimedia.org/wiki/File:Stranded_migrant_workers_during_fourth_phase_of_the_lockdown_IMG_20200523_125500.jpg – Creative Commons licence CC BY-SA 4.0 (https://creativecommons.org/licenses/by-sa/4.0/deed.en).

closed in March 2020 (Figure 4.1). In order to survive, millions of internal migrants returned to their homes in peri-urban and rural areas, walking hundreds of kilometres because other transport links, like buses and trains, had also been shut down.

BOX 4.2 MIGRATION

There is no agreed and singular definition of migration. Instead, there are many different types of migration. As a starting point, migration is the movement of people away from where they usually live. Migration can be internal (within state borders) or international (across state borders). It can be temporary or permanent. It can be forced or voluntary. And migration can sometimes be defined in terms of motivations or causes, such as labour migration (for the purposes of work), student migration (for the purposes of study), or environmental migration (in response to environmental change).

BOX 4.3 MIGRANT

There is no agreed and singular definition of migrant. Instead, there are many different types of migrants. As a starting point, a migrant is a person who has moved away from the place where they usually live. People who move within state borders are called internal migrants. People who move across state borders are called international migrants. Emigrants are migrants defined in terms of the place they are leaving, while immigrants are people who are defined in terms of the place they are moving to. Migrants are often defined in terms of their legal status: legal categories include refugee, asylum seeker, and undocumented. Migrants can also be defined in terms of their attributes, for example skilled migrants.

In this chapter, we explore movement, migration, and mobilities through a number of case studies. In the first case study, we look at the social geographies of migration in more detail. We use the example of internal migration in China, and focus on how it has changed urban and rural places and lives. In the second case study, we consider the mobilities turn. We look at the World Cup in Qatar, and show the types of mobilities that were necessary to allow this event to happen, as well as the consequences. In the third case study, we reflect on the politics of movement. We use a number of different examples to illustrate this. First, we consider how the experiences of disabled people illustrate the politics of movement, mobility, and immobility at local and national scales in particular. Second, we look at the politics of mobility in relation to migration. We show how states create hierarchies of migrants, and how this has impacts on mobility, immobility, and everyday experiences at the international and transnational scales. Though these may seem like very different examples, your task is to think about how these case studies are connected, and what – collectively – they tell us about movement, mobilities, and migration.

II. THE SOCIAL GEOGRAPHIES OF MIGRATION

In 1980, around 20% of the population of China lived in urban areas; by 2020, this proportion had risen to almost 64%.[1] Despite this, most people in China are still officially residents of rural areas, under a population registration system called *hukou*. The *hukou* system was introduced in 1951 and required people to legally register in just one place – either rural or urban. Initially, if a person lived somewhere other than where they registered, they had little or no access to supports such as food or housing or healthcare or education. The result was limited internal migration in China over 30 years. The relaxation of the *hukou* system from the 1980s onwards enabled more internal migration and led to the rapid growth of urban areas. However, the *hukou* system remains in place for access to some services, such as subsidised education and healthcare. Because of this, many residents of Chinese cities – those from rural areas with rural *hukou* – choose to leave their children in their rural home area so they can get access to education.

These migrations to cities, alongside the links with rural areas, can be seen in cities such as Guangzhou. Guangzhou is a city in Southern China, located in the Pearl River Delta. It is a very old settlement that initially developed as a port, though its importance as a port declined from the 1840s onwards. For the next 140 years, the development of Guangzhou was limited. In 1978, its population was less than 2 million. In 1979, however, the Chinese government introduced new economic reforms and a more 'open door' policy, which led to Guangzhou being designated as one of 14 open coastal cities. This allowed the city Guangzhou to expand rapidly, through economic, spatial, and population growth.[2] The current population of Guangzhou is almost 14 million people, an increase of over 600% in 44 years.[3] Much of that growth is driven by migration from other parts of China.

Most of the new residents of Guangzhou – crowded into packed high-rise apartment buildings or company dormitories – have moved there from other parts of China, often from rural areas. They work in the city's factories and offices. Many of these migrants are not officially registered in Guangzhou and may 'float' between the city and less urbanised areas, travelling regularly to the rural area where they grew up or where their family still lives. This means that the migration is ongoing. Rather than a movement 'to' the city, instead it is a mobile existence of moving between places, described as circular migration (Box 4.4).

BOX 4.4 CIRCULAR MIGRATION

Circular migration is the regular movement of a migrant between two different places. Historically, this was called seasonal migration, and it referred to the short-term movement of people to work as agricultural labourers during harvest season. Now, circular migration may be for the purposes of short-term work, but there are other forms, such as people moving from the north to the south of Europe, or from the northern US or Canada to the southern US, during winter, to escape colder weather. Similarly, families from tribal groups in India, such as Gujjars, Gaddis, Bakarwals, and Bhotias, migrate with their livestock between the plains (in winter) and the highland pastures (in summer).

Life for migrants in cities like Guangzhou can be difficult. Researchers describe migrants living in places that are often small, dark, and crowded; working 3D jobs (Box 4.5); and with limited capacity to take part in social activities.[4] Over time, though, some migrants are able to improve their living conditions and employment, and to create a sense of belonging in the city. Others remain connected to their place of origin, and to their rural *hukou*. This may be because of family relations, for example if their spouse or children are still living there, or they have elderly parents that they provide for. Technology can support these relationships, including mobile phones (China has more active mobile phones than people). Transport links also facilitate mobilities between places, where frequent travel may be part of everyday life both within and to and from the city. In these cases, circular migration is common, with migrants moving to and from urban areas on a frequent basis.

BOX 4.5 3D JOBS

The term 3D jobs is used to describe jobs that are Dirty, Dangerous and Difficult/Demanding/Degrading (there is no agreement on what the third D stands for). Examples of 3D jobs include physically difficult agricultural work, or working in overcrowded and unsafe

> factories, or working with toxic materials and manual scavenging. 3D jobs additionally have poor working conditions, such as low pay and precarity. Migrants, particularly those who are from marginalised and/or subordinate caste/class backgrounds, often have no option but to take 3D jobs, which leaves them vulnerable to exploitation, injury and stigmatisation.

The extent of the relationship between cities and rural areas in China is vividly shown each year with *chunyun*, a 40-day travel season associated with the Chinese New Year and the associated Spring Festival. During *chunyun*, workers travel from the cities to their rural homes, in what has been described as the world's largest annual human migration (Figure 4.2). In 2019, there were nearly 3 billion journeys – by road, rail, and airplane – during the period.[5] There is huge demand for travel tickets, and trains are overloaded with people and luggage. Research highlights the difficulties of the journey, including the high cost, physical pain from queuing and from sitting for extended periods on hard seats on trains, and overcrowding. Crang and Zhang describe a train journey as follows: "People were stacked as packages with a suffocating stench filling the carriages. People were reduced to their physical flesh, immobilized to such an extent that they might go without food or drink for 20–30 h to reduce the need to go to the toilet".[6] Despite the expense and the discomfort, *chunyun* is very important for many people, particularly those who are separated from close family.

The rural areas that receive an influx of people during *chunyun* are also changed by migration to the cities. Those who move to cities are mostly young and often male. Because of this, rural areas in China have a large 'left-behind population' of children, women (often spouses) and the elderly – estimated at over 150 million people.[7] This changes the demographic profile of rural areas. It also changes social relations. Some 'left-behind' women may become more autonomous, even though they have additional demands on their time in relation to care work and agricultural work. It can be difficult for 'left-behind' children, separated from one or both parents, or for 'left-behind' elderly parents, forced to take on new responsibilities. However, remittances from migrants can help to

Figure 4.2 Shenzhen North Railway Station Concourse During Chunyun, 2016.

Source: Baycrest, https://commons.wikimedia.org/wiki/File:Shenzhen_North_Railway_Station_Concourse_2016_Chunyun.jpg – Creative commons licence CC BY-SA 2.5 (https://creativecommons.org/licenses/by-sa/2.5/deed.en).

sustain lives and livelihoods in rural areas, so migration is often encouraged despite the emotional costs for both those who leave and those who stay (Box 4.6).

BOX 4.6 REMITTANCES

Remittances are transfers of money from one person to another. While the term can be used in other contexts, it is regularly used in migration studies to describe the money that migrants send to their families and/or communities for everyday or unusual expenses, or to invest in property or businesses in their home area.

Internal migration is changing Chinese cities like Guangzhou. But Guangzhou is also being changed by international migration, both from and to the city. From the 1990s onwards, migrants from the Middle East and African countries have moved to Guangzhou

MOVEMENT, MIGRATION, MOBILITIES **133**

in significant numbers: to study, to trade or to work. This is connected to the intensification of links between China and African
countries in particular. China is now Africa's largest trading part-
ner, and has invested in significant infrastructure projects across
the continent, from ports and roads and dams, to hospitals and
stadia. It's estimated that over one million Chinese nationals now
live in African countries, including professionals, entrepreneurs,
and contract workers.[8] The migrants who move to Guangzhou
from African countries are part of that intensification of links, but
their experiences also illustrate the different effects of migration on
places and people.

Everyday life for African migrants in Guangzhou is often centred in an area colloquially and disparagingly called 'Chocolate
City'. This is one of many urban enclaves in Guangzhou, in this
instance providing shelter and services to African migrants. This is
important in a city where African migrants are regularly racialised
as culturally inferior.[9] In Guangzhou, as in other cities experiencing new forms of migration, there is a tendency to 'other' both
people and places, and to associate newcomers with undesirable
behaviour. Social geographers in particular have long drawn attention to this common practice, which is sometimes related to people's anxieties about change, and sometimes grounded in a belief
in social hierarchies. Importantly, though, urban enclaves also
provide opportunities for positive encounters between migrants
and non-migrants. One example is through food, as Chinese and
Africans mix in restaurants serving African food, Chinese food, or
'Western' food, each offering the possibility of asserting different
identities.[10]

The city of Guangzhou offers one set of insights into the social
geographies of migration. As the city has grown, it has become a
magnet for migrants – often male – from rural China. They have
changed the city, and their migration has also changed their home
areas and their social relations, with families and households separated and stretched over long distances. The connections between
the city and the rural areas are maintained through technology,
through remittances and through visits. The city is also located
in broader global networks that have positioned it as a destination
for international migrants. The movement of people in and out of
Guangzhou, and their experiences at home in the city, highlight the

MOVEMENT, MIGRATION, MOBILITIES

social geographies of migration, and reflect patterns and practices that are common in urban and rural areas around the world.

III. THE MOBILITIES TURN

The 'mobilities turn' has been very influential in social geography, in a variety of ways. It has influenced what social geographers research, and how they do research. It has shown the connections between different types of mobilities and immobilities, and how these are related to space and place (Box 4.7). Traditionally, social geographers have considered certain types of mobilities, like the movement of people through migration or through forms of transportation, often in a quantifiable way. The mobilities turn expanded the range of topics, for example to include the movement of animals or objects, and it also introduced new research methods to social geography (Box 4.8). In particular, it made space for what has been called 'mobile methods': research that is carried out while 'on the move' in order to better understand the experiences of mobility. Mobile methods often make use of new technology, for example wearable technologies. Geographer Tim Cresswell says that when we think about mobility, we need to consider three interconnected aspects. We need to think about physical movement itself; how that movement is represented; and how that movement is embodied or practised.[11] In order to explore these issues in more detail, we will use the example of the Qatar World Cup to learn about the mobilities turn in social geography.

BOX 4.7 THE MOBILITIES TURN

The mobilities turn – sometimes called the new mobilities paradigm – is a new approach to the study of all kinds of mobilities, including people, things, and information. The mobilities turn, which has been growing in influence in the social sciences since the early twenty-first century, is also interested in immobilities: when people, things, and information are unable or not allowed to move. The mobilities turn insists that mobilities and immobilities are a central part of human life, and need to be studied in an interdisciplinary and integrated way.

BOX 4.8 RESEARCH METHODS

Research methods are the tools that are used to carry out research in order to find an answer to a research question. In social geography, traditional research methods include surveys, analysis of census data, and cartographic analysis; in recent years, these research methods have been expanded to include interviews, focus groups, participant observation, action research, and, more recently, mobile methods.

In December 2010, the small Gulf State of Qatar was awarded the right to host the 2022 Men's FIFA World Cup. It was an unexpected decision. In order to host the World Cup, Qatar promised to build new football stadiums, develop local road and rail infrastructure, and ensure that stadiums and transport and public places had effective cooling systems. Qatar was able to make this promise because of its significant wealth from oil and gas, which it exports to countries such as Japan, South Korea, India, and China.[12] The Qatar World Cup illustrates different types of mobilities and immobilities, different mobility infrastructures, and raises important questions about the politics of mobility and the relationship between mobility and place. For instance, a village in Kerala, India, named Kettungal, celebrated the Qatar World Cup in its own way. It is thought that at least one member from each household in the village is a migrant to Qatar and the economy and the village is heavily dependent on the remittances sent.

The state of Qatar gained independence from Britain in 1971; prior to that, it had been a British protectorate. At the time of independence, around 100,000 people lived in Qatar, which is around the size of the US state of Connecticut. Qatar is a very small country, but it has reserves of oil and gas that are estimated to be the third largest in the world. The export of oil and gas and related products, such as polymers and fertilisers, makes Qatar a very wealthy country. Qatar exports these products by pipeline and by sea, and has invested the wealth it has generated widely, including in infrastructure. Qatar's investments in infrastructure have enabled the enhanced mobility of people and things and ideas in a variety of ways. This includes airports, ports, and roads; broadband; the establishment of

MOVEMENT, MIGRATION, MOBILITIES

a state-owned airline (Qatar Airways); and the establishment of a state-owned international media company (Al Jazeera).

Qatar, like its neighbours in the Gulf States, relies heavily on migrant workers to support its economic growth and development. The population of Qatar has grown considerably in the last 50 years: from just over 100,000 people in 1970 to close to 3 million people in 2020.[13] Most of that population growth is from migration. It is estimated that over 85% of the population is foreign-born, with just around 15% of the population who are Qatari nationals.[14] Like other Gulf States, Qatar has strict rules on who can become a citizen. Because of this, its labour market is highly reliant on migrants. Migrant workers in Qatar do all types of jobs: from construction, manufacturing, domestic, and service sector work, to engineering (working in oil and gas), healthcare, and education. Migration to Qatar, and to other Gulf States, usually happens under a sponsorship system known as the *kafala*, where migrants are tied to specific employers, often for a particular period of time. Many migrants get access to a sponsor through an intermediary, known as a labour broker, and pay a considerable fee for a work visa. The *kafala* system leaves migrants vulnerable to exploitation. They may be required to live in unsuitable accommodation provided by their employer, or they may have their salary withheld for dubious reasons (such as 'visa' or 'agent' fees). Many migrant workers in Qatar reported that their passport was held by their employer, which meant that they were effectively trapped in the country until the employer granted them permission to leave.[15] Until recently in Qatar, migrants were unable to change employers or even leave the country without permission from their sponsor.[16]

These different aspects – oil, gas, transportation, ideas, people – all helped to represent Qatar as a modern, mobile, and connected state, and helped to secure Qatar's selection as World Cup host for 2022. Of course, once the decision was made, Qatar had to rapidly invest in new infrastructures, and the development of these infrastructures illustrates many different aspects of mobility. Let's start with the football stadiums needed to host World Cup matches in a country with a limited tradition of soccer. In total, Qatar has built or repurposed eight football stadiums, most of which were designed by international architecture firms. Among the firms who designed stadiums were Foster + Partners, Zaha Hadid Architects, and Fenwick Iribarren Architects, all of which are known for large-scale,

MOVEMENT, MIGRATION, MOBILITIES   **137**

dramatic buildings in locations around the world. This is sometimes called *starchitecture*: the globally-known architects and the spectacular buildings that give places and political leaders a sense of importance. While many of the new stadiums in Qatar make reference to local things, the overarching ideas behind their design are global, showing how information and ideas move from place to place, facilitated by digital communications. This is also an example of the creation of 'globalised' spaces that are the same everywhere in design, 'feel', and use. The stadiums become 'placeless', as they could be anywhere, with the implication that where they are doesn't matter. However, this concept is also challenged by the Qatari example, as new technology was needed specifically for this place in order to create cool environments so that the tournament was feasible for the players. This also required a change of date from the usual month of June to December for the tournament in 2022.[17]

New stadiums may be designed by global firms, but the idea of them as placeless is also problematic when they have to be built in place. This requires mobilities of things and people. There has been a significant importation of raw materials, technology, and expertise. The main port in Qatar – Hamad Port – was expanded to facilitate sea freight and Hamad airport has also expanded its capacity both for the World Cup and the desired tourism increase. More workers were needed for this expansion, with highly-paid elite workers from the Global North designing and managing infrastructure construction, and lower-paid Global South migrants providing physical labour in often difficult conditions. The *Guardian* newspaper reported in 2021 that more than 6,500 migrant workers from India, Pakistan, Nepal, Bangladesh, and Sri Lanka had died in Qatar since December 2010. These figures came from these five countries only and not from the Qatari authorities, so it is likely that the true figure of migrant deaths is much higher. Most of the deaths were reported as 'natural deaths', but human rights campaigners suggest this is unlikely, pointing to the high temperatures in particular as a likely cause.[18]

The temporary mobility of teams and their supporters is an important dimension of any large sporting event. Many cities and countries are eager to stage large sporting events because of a perceived economic benefit from increased tourist numbers both for the event itself and into the future. In the short term, prices for hotels and other accommodation, taxis, food, and other services often increase during events, leading to increased profits. In the longer term, the Qatari establishment is aware of the limitations of their oil and gas revenues as these are finite and is seeking to move away from its reliance on these. There is a desire to develop their tourist industry alongside services, finances, and knowledge-based economy to create more sustainable sources of income.[19] The hope is that the visibility and prestige of the events will attract tourists in the future. These ambitions rely on developing the reputation of the country. In order to make the World Cup a success, in addition to the development of tourist infrastructure all kinds of additional goods will need to be brought into Qatar, such as food and drink. Alcohol posed a problem, because the consumption of alcohol in Qatar is generally highly regulated, in contrast to the regular practice at other large-scale sporting events. It was not possible for fans to purchase alcohol at the stadium. Instead, fans were permitted to purchase and drink alcohol in designated zones, while also being warned against public drunkenness. While LGBTQI+ fans were assured they were welcome, Qatar represses the rights of LGBTQI+ citizens and residents, with same-sex conduct punishable by up to seven years in prison. National teams and fans were banned from displaying symbols in support of LGBTQI+ rights, such as 'OneLove' armbands or rainbow flags. In order to make the World Cup a success in the eyes of potential tourists, Qatar effectively distinguished between the rights of residents and the rights of mobile non-residents, creating new spaces and places in the process. In Qatar's hosting of the World Cup, they sought to show the country as a thriving and exciting tourist (and finance) destination and 'wash' over the treatment of migrants who built the infrastructures that make the event possible, and the treatment of residents and citizens who do not conform to norms around sexual identity and practice (Box 4.9).

BOX 4.9 SPORTS-WASHING

Sports-washing is where a country, company, organisation, group, or individual seeks to use sport to 'clean' up their reputation. This can be through sponsoring or hosting an event, financially supporting a team or by engaging in sport itself and seeking to win medals. In this way, they seek to be associated with sport rather than the social, environmental, or other activity that they have engaged in and are known for.

These hybrid geographies of people, things and ideas create the spectacle of the World Cup and the landscapes of Qatar in temporary and more residual ways. If we return to Tim Cresswell's suggestions for how geographers should think about mobility, we can see the physical movement of oil and gas, and of the things and people needed to build infrastructure. We can see how the movement is embodied or practised, in the bodies of migrant labourers or partying football supporters, as well as in the bodies of elite architects and professionals. And we can see how movement is represented, with the movement of oil and gas and tourists enabled and encouraged by the Qatari state, while activists use this temporary openness to spread information about the treatment of migrant workers and LGBTQI+ residents internationally in order to effect changes in place. The event of the World Cup, with its connections to past, current, and present mobilities of people, things and information, offers an excellent example of how the mobilities turn helps social geographers better understand the relationship between people and places.

IV. THE POLITICS OF MOVEMENT

The mobilities turn has insisted on the importance of studying both mobility and immobility. Who and what gets to move, and who and what doesn't get to move, are important questions for social geographers to consider. We want to consider the politics of movement in two interconnected ways. First, we want to consider the relationship between disability and mobility. Second, we want to look in more detail at migration. Both of these examples offer important insights into both mobilities and immobilities. We use them to draw attention to and reflect on who gets to move, and who gets 'stuck', in our world. This is sometimes described as 'mobility justice', and we will return to this at the end of this section.

Many of us expect to be able to move around our environment without restrictions. We assume we will be able to use different forms of transport, to go in and out of buildings, and to move freely in public spaces. However, there are social groups for whom mobility is more complicated. Parents with children may face obstacles to using public transport. Older people may be wary of moving around places that are steep or have slippery surfaces. Children often experience restrictions on mobility. Racial or ethnic minorities or women

140 MOVEMENT, MIGRATION, MOBILITIES

may be confined in their movements because of the threat of abuse or assault.[20] For many disabled people, restrictions on mobility may be even more widespread, because of how our built environments and infrastructures are designed. This has been described as 'disabling environments' (Box 4.10). Who can or cannot move is created through landscapes and infrastructure (Figure 4.3).

BOX 4.10 DISABLING ENVIRONMENTS

Disabling environments sees places, environment, and structures of society as disabling rather than understanding someone as being 'at fault' for not being 'able' to undertake specific tasks or go particular places. This is true for both physical environments and infrastructure that can constrain safe movement within and between places, and also social spaces that mean people are overwhelmed, confused, or cannot engage in them in ways that others can. In some cases, physical environments and their creation are regulated by laws that ensure that new buildings need to be accessible in terms of lifts/doors/toilets, while public transport is often required to have specific seats/spaces set aside for people who need help accessing the environment that has been constructed for people who are enabled to participate fully in it. These however can be limited in understanding disabilities and accessibility as only those who use wheelchairs and may not account for other visible and invisible disabilities.

Social geographers have paid considerable attention to how the mobility of disabled people is restricted through disabling environments. Earlier work focused on the experiences of people with particular types of physical disabilities, such as visual impairment or blindness. This demonstrated how the actions of others, for example, parking on a footpath, new street furniture, or road works, created significant obstacles to the easy movement in public space of people with visual impairments.[21] People who use wheelchairs also report a range of ways in which the actions of others – evident in both the design and the use of environments – contributed to their restricted mobility. Some of the examples include discontinuous routeways, uneven surfaces, pavements without dropped kerbs,

MOVEMENT, MIGRATION, MOBILITIES   141

Figure 4.3 Sign Warning People in Wheelchairs of a Steep Slope in Dublin, Ireland.

Source: Authors' Photograph.

poorly designed bus stops, heavy doors, steps, and stairs without ramps. These examples focus on more visible or recognisable physical disabilities. More recent work has focused on how environments disable other groups, such as people with learning disabilities who reported feeling unsafe or unsettled in public spaces and who developed mobility and immobility strategies to cope. For example, Ed Hall and Ellie Bates used walking interviews to better understand the experiences and practices of people with learning disabilities. They found examples of people "moving through the city as quickly as possible, avoiding spaces and encounters of perceived anxiety and uncertainty", as well as retreating to quiet spaces for rest, to escape sensory overload, and to avoid particular groups of people.[22] Disabling environments have also been reported by fat people, for example when travelling by plane.[23] As airlines seek to maximise profit by carrying more passengers on flights, seat sizes have been made smaller and less comfortable. This not only creates more discomfort for fat people; it also serves to embody overcrowding in the bodies of fat people rather than in the decisions of corporations.

The politics of mobility is thus clearly evident in disabling environments. It is possible for us to develop built environments and infrastructure that are more inclusive and enable mobility if we are attentive to the needs of diverse users. By persisting with disabling environments, we are creating hierarchies of mobility. Our built environments and infrastructure enable unfettered mobility for some, restricted mobility for others, and inhibit mobility entirely for a small minority. Even when laws and policies are in place to protect mobility rights, practice can undermine them. For example, Mary and Kath live in Ireland where, even though it is illegal to discriminate against people on the basis of disability, disabled people often report that they have significant difficulties getting a taxi or getting on to public buses or trains. In the building where Mary works, there is a chairlift to allow people with impaired mobility to get to the geography department on the second floor, but it is often out of order, as is the mechanism that enables the heavy external door to open automatically. These experiences show that mobility is not an everyday right for many people, and the decisions that limit their mobility are political. They serve to create and maintain inclusive built environments and infrastructure for some people and not for others.

Borders are also a form of infrastructure that restrict or prevent mobility for some, while enabling it for others. Borders can exist at a whole range of scales: here, we are particularly interested in national borders that separate one country from another. The border between the US and Mexico is notorious. Former President Donald Trump made building and reinforcing a border wall between the two countries one of the key aims of his presidency, with the express aim of keeping Mexican and other Central and South American migrants out of the US. There has been a rapid growth in national border wall building in recent years, all designed to restrict the mobility of the 'wrong' kinds of migrants. Between Mexico and the US, just as between virtually every other bordering countries there are also express routes through borders for favoured travellers or migrants, and for goods passing from one place to the other. In a globalised world, the control of the movement of people

MOVEMENT, MIGRATION, MOBILITIES **143**

through its borders is one of the few ways in which a state can show its power and influence. That control is expressed through the creation of hierarchies of undesirable and desirable people – based on their nationality, skills, family relationships, and other aspects of social identity.

One group of migrants that is often seen as undesirable is refugees and asylum seekers (Box 4.11). Under international law, countries have a responsibility to provide protection to refugees. Many religious and ethical codes also recognise this responsibility. However, there is an important social geography to the varied responses to different groups of refugees and asylum seekers. Most refugees and asylum seekers are cared for in neighbouring countries. Wealthy countries – often far removed from the direct effects of wars or conflicts that give rise to the mass movement of people – place conditions and restrictions on who they accept as refugees, and treat many of those seeking asylum with suspicion.

BOX 4.11 REFUGEES AND ASYLUM SEEKERS

In general terms, both refugees and asylum seekers have fled their homes because of fears for their safety. These two terms are sometimes used interchangeably, but there is a difference in their legal meaning. Legally, a refugee is a person who has been recognised in international law as not being able to return to their home country because of a "well-founded fear of being persecuted" because of their "race, religion, nationality, membership of a particular social group, or political opinion".[24] An asylum seeker is a person who is looking to be recognised as a refugee.

When Russia invaded Ukraine in 2022, many people fled the country because of their fears of death and injury. In response, the EU activated its Temporary Protection Directive. The Directive was agreed in 2001, but this is the first time it has been activated. It means that Ukrainian nationals can live and work in the EU without a visa for at least one year, and can have access to social benefits such as housing and healthcare. However, the Directive only applies to Ukrainian nationals. Nationals of countries from outside the EU, like the international students living in Ukraine from countries like India and Morocco and Nigeria, are not covered.[25] In the early days of the war, there were reports from the border between Poland and Ukraine of African and Asian students being refused entry to Poland.[26] Yet all the people fleeing Ukraine, regardless of their nationality, are leaving because of the same threats from bombing and fighting and the destruction of lives and homes and infrastructure. Their different treatment at the border, based on their nationality, clearly shows the politics of movement at work. Similarly, the treatment of Ukrainian refugees in the EU has been contrasted with the treatment of Syrian refugees. Though also fleeing war, Syrians did not receive automatic temporary protection in the EU, and so had to apply individually for refugee status which was not always granted. In this way, we see how particular groups, from particular places, are considered more deserving of the right to move and make a new, safe home than others.

Nationality gives some people extensive mobility rights. The Henley Passport Index ranks passports based on the number of countries a holder can travel to without a visa. Citizens of Japan top the list: in 2022, they could travel to 193 countries visa-free. Irish citizens, like Kath and Mary, are able to travel to 187 countries without a visa. In contrast, Indian citizens, like Dhiren and Niharika, can avail of visa-free travel to just 60 countries. Only 27 countries will admit Afghan citizens without a visa.[27] People also have access to mobility rights through 'skills'. Many countries are keen to attract particular types of so-called 'highly skilled' migrants. The definition of highly skilled is context-dependent: it depends on what skills are in demand in particular places, and it is often connected to high salary levels. As an example, many health professionals, such as doctors, are generally understood as highly skilled. In 2022, butchers and bakers were described as highly skilled in the UK, because of a shortage of workers after the UK's exit from the EU. At the same time, in Ireland, butchers and bakers were not considered highly skilled. When people are considered highly skilled, their migration is actively encouraged so they can work in their area of expertise. Highly skilled migrants often have more favourable visa conditions, more rights, and quicker routes to citizenship than other migrants, who are considered less skilled. In particular, highly skilled migrants are often able to ensure that members of their family also have access to mobility rights. The types of family relationships that are prioritised are heteronormative: husbands and wives; parents and young children. It is less likely that same-sex

MOVEMENT, MIGRATION, MOBILITIES   **145**

couples or a broader range of family members, such as grandparents or siblings, will be given mobility rights in this way. Queer and trans asylum seekers often are caught in the complex web of global politics and migration. Scholars have argued that certain countries are homophobic, which in turn creates a divide between the worst places to be gay and the safest places which are often situated in the West. However, while their sexuality may be more accepted in the West, queer and trans asylum seekers face other struggles, such as being treated with suspicion or hostility on the basis on their nationality or religion, or the challenges of economic survival. In this context, if queer or trans asylum seekers are pushed to produce an overarching Islamophobic narrative of their oppression, for example, what does this tell us about the broader politics of mobility?

We want to illustrate how the practice of creating hierarchies of migrants illustrates the politics of mobility, by showing how this enables both movement and 'stuckness'. We want to look at a particular group of migrants: those who move from one country to another for the purposes of caring work. Care work takes many forms. It could involve looking after people who are unable to look after themselves: babies and children, older people, people who are ill or who have a disability that restricts their independence. It might involve preparing food, or helping people with personal hygiene, or washing clothes or cleaning. Education can be seen as a form of care work, as can health care and providing emotional support for people. Care work is an example of social reproduction (Box 4.12).

BOX 4.12 SOCIAL REPRODUCTION

Social reproduction refers to the structures and work that are necessary to allow society to continue, such as education and healthcare and public transport and childcare. The term is often used by Marxist feminists[28] to argue that capitalist production and the accumulation of profits is only possible because of social reproduction work that is often done by women.

Care work is provided *in situ* – in the places where people need care. Increasingly, the workers who provide care come from other places, because of changes in the social geographies of Western countries in particular. In many Western countries, there is a crisis of care.

In the past, women working in the home would have been responsible for much care work, such as looking after children or older people. In most cases, this care work was unpaid. Now, women are more likely to work outside the home, which means there are fewer people available or willing to do the work of care. Care needs have increased, because Western societies are aging: the median age in the European Union in 2020 was 43.9 years, compared to 38.4 years in 2001. And this work is now more likely to be paid work, rather than done for free by family members as in the past. This is the crisis of care: more care is needed, but there are fewer people available to provide it.

In order to fill this gap, Western countries have turned to migrants. A range of migration schemes have been designed to make it easier for people – usually women – to move to Western countries in order to work as carers. Canada provides an excellent example, with its Live-In Caregiver Programme (LCP). The LCP allowed Canadian families to bring a foreign national into Canada to work as a caregiver in a private household.[29] Most of the caregivers who moved to Canada under this programme were Filipina women. Like the construction workers in Qatar, they were temporary migrants. Many were mothers of children who remained in the Philippines, cared for by their other parent or grandparents or by members of their extended family. This gives rise to an international division of reproductive labour that is based on people's access to mobility rights (Box 4.13). Filipina migrants care for people in Canada, earning money that they send to family members in the Philippines, who in turn care for the migrants' children. Children are 'stuck' in the Philippines because they cannot legally migrate with their parent; people with care needs are 'stuck' in their homes in Canada; and they are linked by the migrant who moves to Canada and who connects the two places through communications, remittances and travel.

BOX 4.13 INTERNATIONAL DIVISION OF REPRODUCTIVE LABOUR

Migration scholar Rhacel Parreñas developed this concept based on her research with Filipina migrants. She showed how, under global capitalism, reproductive activities in one country – for example care

> work, household chores – are connected to reproductive activities in another area. As she describes it, the international division of reproductive labour means that migrant workers do the reproductive labour of privileged women in industrialised countries, while the reproductive labour of migrant workers in their home country is carried out by those who are unable to move. This concept was later renamed as the 'global care chain' by Parreñas's PhD supervisor.

Generally, care work is not treated as highly skilled work, even though there is huge demand for caregivers across industrialised and wealthy countries. This may be because care work is often associated with women, and women's work is rarely seen as highly skilled. The LCP was unusual, because it provided a route to more permanent residence in Canada for migrants and their immediate families, thus acknowledging that care work was skilled work. After two years working as a live-in caregiver, a migrant could apply for permanent residency and sponsor their families to join them. Many people participated in the LCP for this reason, as it allowed them to move beyond temporary status and build a new home in Canada, though in practice there were long delays because of state limits on how many people could get permanent residence each year. However, it's important to realise that for those two years, caregivers were also 'stuck', tied to one employer and required to live in their employer's home. Their children were also 'stuck', unable to move to Canada to be with their parent. Despite this, the Canadian LCP scheme offered more rights to care workers than many other countries. Experiences elsewhere show that migrant care workers, particularly those required to live with their employers, are often subject to abuse and/or assault. They are often unable to avail of broader social or legal protections because their workplace is thought of primarily as a home for other people, rather than a place of work. Care work is based on, and results in, social and spatial differences and hierarchies linked to the politics of mobility.

All of these different examples point to the concept of 'mobility justice', which draws our attention to who and what gets to move and under what conditions (Box 4.14). Our examples show mobility justice and injustice at a range of scales. Disabling environments point to the ways some people's movement through our built environments is restricted. Borders show how states restrict the movement of some while enabling the movement of others. Migration for care work shows the complicated hierarchies of mobility that are linked through the international division of reproductive labour. In all of these examples, our concern as social geographers is the power relations that give some people mobility rights in and across some places, while restricting the mobility rights of others.

> ### BOX 4.14 MOBILITY JUSTICE
>
> Mobility justice is concerned with who has access to mobility, who has not, and the power structures that underpin this differential access. It considers experiences of mobility and immobility at a range of scales, from the body to the nation-state and the world. By drawing attention to the processes that result in differential social and spatial access to mobility, it seeks to improve access to mobility for all.[30]

V. CONCLUSION

In this chapter, we discussed how movement and place influence each other. We used a range of examples to illustrate this relationship. First, we discussed internal migration in China. With a particular focus on the city of Guangzhou, we showed how migration changes rural areas, urban areas, and social relations. Next, we introduced you to the mobilities turn, which expands how we think about movement to include things and information, in addition to people. We used the 2022 World Cup in Qatar as an example, and described all the different types of mobilities – for example, oil and gas, migrant workers, ideas about the design of built environments, raw materials for building projects, and teams and supporters – that are necessary for the event to take place. Finally, we discussed the politics of mobility, paying attention to both mobility *and* immobility. We considered the relationship between disability and im/mobility, and the ways in which our built environment makes it difficult for people with disabilities to be mobile. We also looked at the politics of migration, and the ways in which states enable the movement of some people, and make the movement of others much more difficult, whether through borders, passports, or visa regimes.

This chapter contains a diverse range of examples, but these examples are linked together by their concern with the relationship between movement and place. Social geography is concerned with social lives that are made in space and place, and that in turn shape the spaces and places where they exist. Movement – whether of people, things, or ideas – is a central part of social life, and shapes spaces and places in a variety of ways, from depopulated rural areas to newly constructed urban landscapes. However, the chapter also draws our attention to the contested politics of movement, and to the ways in which movement, or mobility, is a resource with unequal access. For some, movement is easy and unproblematic. For others, movement is difficult or indeed impossible. As social geographers, it is important that we consider immobility as well as mobility, and its relationship with space and place. Our social world is, and will continue to be, shaped by movement. Understanding who and what gets to move, and on what terms, will help us to better understand the role of movement in our social lives, and to see the potential of movement for building better lives.

NOTES

1 Chan, K. W. (2021) "Internal migration in China: Integrating migration with Urbanization policies and Hokou reform". *KNOMAD Policy Brief 16*, November 2021. Available online at www.knomad.org/publication/internal-migration-china-integrating-migration-urbanization-policies-and-hukou-reform.

2 Xu, J. and A. G. O. Yeh (2003) "Guangzhou". *Cities* 20(5): 361–374.

3 Available from https://worldpopulationreview.com/world-cities/guangzhou-population. For comparison, the population of London and New York increased by 38% and 9% respectively in the same period.

4 Suda, K. (2016) "A room of one's own: Highly educated migrants' strategies for creating a *home* in Guangzhou". *Population, Space and Place* 22(2): 146–157. https://doi.org/10.1002/psp.1898.

5 Mu, X., A. G.-O. Yeh and X. Zhang (2021) "The interplay of spatial spread of COVID-19 and human mobility in the urban system of China during the Chinese New Year". *Environment and Planning B: Urban Analytics and City Science* 48(7): 1955–1971. https://doi.org/10.1177/2399808320954211.

MOVEMENT, MIGRATION, MOBILITIES

6 Crang, M. and J. Zhang (2012) "Transient dwelling: Trains as places of identification for the floating population of China". *Social & Cultural Geography* 13(8): 895–914. https://doi.org/10.1080/14649365.2012.728617.

7 Ye, J. (2018) "Stayers in China's 'hollowed-out' villages: A counter narrative on massive rural-urban migration". *Population, Space and Place* 24(4): e2128. https://doi.org/10.1002/psp.2128.

8 Sullivan, J. and J. Cheng (2018) "Contextualising Chinese migration to Africa". *Journal of Asian and African Studies* 53(8): 1173–1187. https://doi.org/10.1177/0021909618776443.

9 Castillo, R. (2014) "Feeling at home in the 'Chocolate City': An exploration of place-making practices and structures of belonging amongst Africans in Guangzhou". *Inter-Asia Cultural Studies* 15(2): 235–257. https://doi.org/10.1080/14649373.2014.911513; Liang, K. and P. Le Billon (2020) "African migrants in China: Space, race and embodied encounters in Guangzhou, China". *Social & Cultural Geography* 21(5): 602–628. https://doi.org/10.1080/14649365.2018.1514647.

10 Ho, E. L.-E. (2018) "African student migrants in China: Negotiating the global geographies of power through gastronomic practices and culture". *Food, Culture & Society* 21(1): 9–24. https://doi.org/10.1080/15528014.2017.1398468.

11 Cresswell, T. (2010) "Towards a politics of mobility". *Environment and Planning D: Society and Space* 28: 17–31.

12 Profile of Qatar by OEC (The Observatory of Economic Complexity). Available online at https://oec.world/en/profile/country/qat.

13 Available from https://worldpopulationreview.com/countries/qatar-population.

14 Seshan, G. (2012) "Migrants in Qatar: A socio-economic profile". *Journal of Arabian Studies* 2(2): 157–171. https://doi.org/10.1080/21534764.2012.735458.

15 Gardner, A., S. Pessoa, A. Diop, K. Al-Ghanim, K. Le Trung and L. Harkness (2013) "A portrait of low-income migrants in contemporary Qatar". *Journal of Arabian Studies* 3(1): 1–17. https://doi.org/10.1080/21534764.2013.806076.

16 Babar, Z., M. Ewers and N. Khattab (2019) "Im/mobile highly skilled migrants in Qatar". *Journal of Ethnic and Migration Studies* 45(9): 1553–1570. https://doi.org/10.1080/1369183X.2018.1492372.

17 Average temperatures in Qatar in June are around 42°C (maximum) and 29°C (minimum). There were concerns that many footballers would be unable to cope with these temperatures. The December average temperatures are around 25°C (maximum) and 16°C (minimum), which are more conducive to strenuous physical activity.

18 Pattisson, P. et al. (2021) "Revealed: 6,500 migrant workers have died in Qatar since World Cup awarded". *The Guardian*, 23 February. Available online at www.theguardian.com/global-development/2021/feb/23/revealed-migrant-worker-deaths-qatar-fifa-world-cup-2022.

19 Morakabati, Y., J. Beavis and J. Fletcher (2014) "Planning for a Qatar without oil: Tourism and economic diversification, a battle of perceptions". *Tourism Planning & Development* 11(4): 415–434. https://doi.org/10.1080/21568316.2014.884978s.

20 Imrie, R. (2000) "Disability and discourses of mobility and movement". *Environment and Planning A* 32(9): 1641–1656.

21 Kitchin, R.M., D. Jacobson, R. G. Golledge and M. Blades (1998) "Belfast without sight: Exploring geographies of blindness". *Irish Geography* 31(1): 34–46. https://doi.org/10.1080/00750779809478630.

22 Hall, E. and E. Bates (2019) "Hatescape? A relational geography of disability hate crime, exclusion and belonging in the city". *Geoforum* 101: 100–110. https://doi.org/10.1016/j.geoforum.2019.02.024.

23 Evans, B., S. Bias and R. Colls (2021) "The dys-appearing fat body: Bodily intensities and fatphobic sociomaterialities when flying while fat". *Annals of the American Association of Geographers* 111(6): 1816–1832. https://doi.org/10.1080/24694452.2020.1866485.

24 The internationally and legally accepted definition of refugee is contained in the 1951 Refugee Convention. You can read it here: www.unhcr.org/en-ie/what-is-a-refugee.html.

25 Hladchenko, M. (2021) "International students in Ukraine: A gateway to developed countries". *European Journal of Higher Education*. https://doi.org/10.1080/21568235.2021.1988669.

26 Akinwotu, E. and W. Strzyżyńska (2022) "Nigeria condemns treatment of Africans trying to flee Ukraine". *The Guardian*, 28 February. Available online at www.theguardian.com/world/2022/feb/28/nigeria-condemns-treatment-africans-trying-to-flee-ukraine-government-poland-discrimination.

27 Read about the Henley Passport Index at www.henleyglobal.com/passport-index/ranking.

28 Marxist feminists draw from Karl Marx's studies of oppression in capitalism to talk about how women form an oppressed class in a patriarchal society. Some notable Marxist feminists are Alexandra Kollontai (1872–1952) and Angela Davis (1944–).

29 Pratt, G. (2012) *Families Apart: Migrant Mothers and the Conflicts of Labour and Love*. Minneapolis: University of Minnesota Press.

30 Sheller, M. (2018) "Theorising mobility justice". *Tempo Social* 30(2): 17–34. Available online at www.scielo.br/j/ts/i/2018.v30n2/.

FURTHER READING

BOOKS

Adey, P. (2017) *Mobility* (2nd ed.). London and New York: Routledge.

Gilmartin, M., P. Burke Wood and C. O'Callaghan (2018) *Borders, Mobility and Belonging*. London: Policy Press.

Jones, R. (2016) *Violent Borders: Refugees and the Right to Move*. London: Verso.

Mitchell, K., R. Jones and J. Fluri (eds.) (2019) *Handbook on Critical Geographies of Migration*. Cheltenham: Edward Elgar Publishing.

Pratt, G. (2012) *Families Apart: Migrant Mothers and the Conflicts of Labour and Love*. Minneapolis: University of Minnesota Press.

Samers, M. and M. Collyer (2017) *Migration* (2nd ed.). London and New York: Routledge.

Walia, H. (2013) *Undoing Border Imperialism*. Oakland, CA: AK Press.

JOURNALS

Mobilities. Available online at www.tandfonline.com/journals/rmob 20

Population, Space and Place. Available online at https://onlinelibrary.wiley.com/journal/15448452

OTHER RESOURCES

International Organisation for Migration (2023) *Key Migration Terms*. Available online at www.iom.int/key-migration-terms

International Organisation for Migration (2023) *Migration Data Portal*. Available online at www.migrationdataportal.org/resources

CONCLUSION
Concluding dialogue

I. INTRODUCTION

Geographers are located in different places; we create knowledge in different ways. As an example, seeking to extend the racial politics of the US to other places needs to carefully consider and respect the different power relations and struggles that exist elsewhere, such as caste-based politics in India. In discussing these issues, we can show that how, where, and who we are means that we look at, come at, and think about social geographies in different ways.

We have various priorities and considerations, all of which are valid and do not need to be hierarchised. Indeed, which politics, inequalities, and social justice initiatives are important will vary depending on where we are. As social geographers (to various extents), we, the authors of this book, see this subject field as important for hope, through contesting social norms and inequalities to create tools for change. Spatial lenses rework how we understand social lives, identities, and experiences. Therefore, it is important to know which views are privileged in order to reject a sole view from the centre, challenge the romanticisation of pre-colonial pasts, and think about how ideas and knowledge can be picked up and used in socially regressive ways.

We now invite you, the reader, to listen to a conversation between the authors.[1] We will explore our journeys into social geographies, and encourage you to think about what leads you here and what might be next; we then consider the place and importance of social geographies and offer 'tools' that you might consider for social change. We do not write as one, because we want to show you how

DOI: 10.4324/9781003266877-6

Figure 5.1 Drawing Representing Zoom Call Dialogue among Authors on Possible Social Geographies.

Source: Illustration by Prateek Draik.

thinking and priorities differ, to allow you the space to consider your place, and the place you are in, for both learning about social geographies, and also applying the critiques of power inherent to social geographies to make change.

Our conversation starts with our journeys to social geography. We then explore the messiness of social geographies, before looking at how we play with and change strict borders and boundaries around what social geographies are or might be. Finally, we turn to considerations for the future, a future we envisage as being co-created with you as the readers of this book and with those who seek to advance positive social change where you are.

II. ACCIDENTAL GEOGRAPHERS: OUR JOURNEYS WITH SOCIAL GEOGRAPHY

MARY: It occurred to me that we write about our different positionalities but we've never actually been explicit about them. Would it be helpful as part of this book for us to reflect a little on our own position, our own training, the gaps in the way that we think about social geography, the context where we learned social geography and what we're fighting against and what we're fighting with? I think it's interesting and I think it would be good for us. I mean, I was very conscious of writing a draft of the introduction and just realising I knew so little about social geography in other contexts. I think we need to own our own ignorance.

Okay I'll start since I was the person talking about it, so I was an accidental geographer. When I went to university, geography was not something I had planned to study. In my undergraduate degree programme I had to pick three subjects, and geography was my third subject. I became really interested in it because of one person who taught me, Anne Buttimer, who was a humanistic geographer and really cared about the social aspect; so that was my introduction to social geography. Really, though, I was trained in a very traditional Irish geography department, where the emphasis was on historical geography and cultural geography and the historical and cultural came together. For most people in the department, social geography was about the divisions in Northern Ireland during the Troubles, and they didn't really see much beyond that. So social geography was not a large part of my undergraduate training, and it wasn't that large a part of my postgraduate training either. I moved to the University of Kentucky for postgrad training, and I got there just with the turn to post-modernism and post-structuralism. So, my Master's and PhD training was very much influenced by social theory, more broadly, not by social geography in particular. Social geography is quite marginal within the US anyway, and is probably more dominant in Europe than it is in the US. I think, as I developed, I found it difficult at times to see a difference between social and cultural geography. I find a lot of the divisions between subdisciplines in human geography not that helpful. They're much more about disciplinary distinctions rather than about understanding the key issues and problems and processes that I think we as geographers should be concerned with. And I think that those key issues and processes are really about questions of power and inequality and justice and injustice. This is what brought me back to social geography in the end; those concerns with how the world is unjust and how we might imagine a different type of world. This is where the social geography tools come in. So that, I think, is social geography.

DHIREN: I also came to geography by accident. Though looking back, it feels, I always knew how our lives were invariably coded through our geographies. Where we lived to what worlds we could imagine and dream. I was the first in my family to complete schooling, and my family's social and economic constraints did not promise going beyond high school. At best, what I aspired to was to be a primary school teacher. It was the maximum anybody from my community had ever achieved (until then). It was the benchmark of success and also respect. Both my parents were working class. My father, a waiter; and my mother, a domestic help. And most of our lives we lived in a caste coded neighbourhood. Interspersed by my queerness that made 'querious' (queer curious) connections with all these social realities. Pushing me to think outside, asking me to escape beyond these contexts. It is interesting how for many of us even dreams come with spatial limits.

CONCLUSION 157

I might have come formally to social geography much later when I came to Delhi for my post-graduation, and yet retrospectively, I feel I was always meant to do this. It was a sheer accident and it was because of some big sacrifices from my family that I could do my undergraduate studies from a small government college in a nearby town in Rajasthan. Also, that public education was cheap, and mildly affordable. I had scored really well in geography in my twelfth standard (taken at 18 to finish school), and thought I could do better in this field. (Everything else that I dreamed of as a vocation, be it law, journalism, or fashion designing, was either unimaginable or unaffordable.) There was no provision of geography as a major in my college and it was one of the three subjects I studied, along with Economics and English Literature. While the college did not have many permanent faculties and remained understaffed through the period of my study, with rare availability of books, my training in social geography began mostly outside the classroom. Inside the class we were only trained in physical geography.

The college represented a specific social grouping; mostly comprising Dalit and Adivasi students from nearby villages and many dominant castes (mostly men). The first question when you enter college would usually be about your caste, and such would also define who your possible friends could be (social circles) and what spaces you could inhabit (social spaces).

For me, to just access this college space was a social intervention and a geographical leap. It was here I was suggested by a young adjunct professor in geography to expand my spatial horizon and think of Delhi. My command over the English language was slightly better than my classmates (even the dominant castes), and this teacher felt this could be my key to success and breaking barriers. My broken English would often encourage upper-caste boys to cross caste barriers and speak to me. It was for me also a lesson in desire. It felt strangely empowering and yet solidified our service to coloniality. It was believed this would help me in clearing the entrance examination to one of the most prestigious social science universities in the country. Apart from caste and class, here I learned how language was used to gatekeep the social production of knowledge and thus power.

Accidentally again (for how merit is usually produced to privilege demonstrable skills associated with dominant classes, and I could barely camouflage my existence outside of this), I cleared this entrance exam. The distance between the capital city of Delhi and my home town was not merely physical in nature but social and economic. My grandmother was apprehensive about sending any of the children to the big city. We had stories and myths suggesting how people from our communities who go out to study are consumed by these cities. We don't survive. We are bullied, killed, or commit suicide. News and stories from across the country kept reaffirming the same.

It was after much convincing from an upper-caste friend (lover), that my parents agreed to send me. This was also a negotiation of power. How the words of my rich, upper-caste lover had more convincing power than my relentless persuasion. The less than three dollars a semester tuition fee at Jawaharlal Nehru University, where I was to study, also helped in this decision. It was prestigious and cheap. We felt it was our step to upward mobility, a timid attempt to claim some respect.

The classroom here was full of gold medalists from fancy universities across India. I felt out of place. Questioning at every step what I was doing here. I sense so many of us even today, as we speak of decolonising the academy, struggle to belong. I still remember the same question that we are discussing right now posed at this university on my first day – 'introduce yourself'. Soon after I mentioned the non-descript college I studied in, I was paraded across the department from one faculty to another, much like a specimen. They said it was rare that I was here and they didn't expect anyone else from my place to be here. Despite our claims for social and spatial diversities in our campuses – and my university claimed to be a bastion of such revolutionary ideas – the imagination of the futures of such places are so limiting. It perplexed me whether I should feel grateful and proud for making it here, or rather sorry for the contexts I came from.

Unlike what Mary was saying about how Irish departments were obsessed with historical and cultural geography, my university department was/is obsessed with social geography. In contrast to other departments in the country like in Kolkata, which was another seat of geographical knowledge production focussing on geomorphology, we were all about social geography. The person who started the department recruited people specifically trained in social geography or sister disciplines. Aijazuddin Ahmed, who introduced the course on social geography and taught at my institution way before I was to join it as a student, also produced the first textbook on social geography in India. It was more in terms of descriptive and distributive aspects of contemporary empirical research on social processes and socialisation in India and their geographical roots. The chapterisation had more conventional divisions in terms of caste, tribe, religion, and so on.

I was trained into that kind of social geography, which then also made me challenge some of these frameworks within the department when I started doing queer work. I had extremely supportive supervisors in this journey. However, there were others who found this unpalatable, less rigorous, something new. They said, 'Okay fine we do social geographies, but what is this that you're bringing in now?' It didn't fit into their conventional listing of the ways in which social is constituted. I would challenge them saying 'but sexual is so significant in all of these constitutions that you're talking about in the classroom'. So while the department allowed my research, it was also very difficult in the sense that you would often be cornered by a senior professor who taught social geography. He brought in discussions on Gramsci and cultural hegemony in the classroom but would outside of it blatantly refer to me as 'hey LGBT' or ask 'how my animal rights were going'?

We are space invaders continuously challenging these spaces. Our presence in these departments – the temples of knowledge production and change – is already a resistance. We redefine the social in the social geographies that are drawn and studied and ways in which these knowledges are produced. It is a continuous conversation, a dialogue, though, which will face contestation, will actually enable vibrant new geographical knowledge to be produced. Currently there are few more scholars in the geography department at Jawaharlal Nehru University (JNU) and University of Delhi working on queerness which brings joy.

I am very excited to be 'accidentally' here. I wanted to be a fashion designer or maybe a journalist, or maybe a lawyer. But because I scored very good marks in the 12th in geography, I thought 'Okay, fine, I can be a schoolteacher at least studying geography'. But because the education was so cheap, 'yeah okay, I can do my PhD'. And today, I am here writing this book alongside such spectacular

160 CONCLUSION

and generous scholars, thinking collectively how we can start thinking of untapped ways of reading, living, defining social geographies and imagining possible change.

NIHARIKA: As you know I am not a trained geographer unlike you three. The closest that I came to in getting interested in social geography via questions of place and space was through a course on urban sociology that I opted for during my PhD studies in Buffalo, New York. My PhD work was made possible by a teaching assistantship that I had received. I was very excited for this opportunity as, more than studies, it allowed me to cross my familiar geographical borders and see a new place. But I was also very anxious as I could not speak English very well and I was afraid how much of a barrier that would be.

Very early on in the semester, I encountered an obstacle that while rooted in my unfamiliarity with a place was also about geopolitical geographical hierarchies. In one urban sociology class, my teacher, who was a well-known urban sociologist, very directly passed a patronising comment. He said that he was glad that I was there to learn from him as I could not write. My term paper was about de-industrialisation in Buffalo, which was my entry point into learning about the political economy of place. But that quickly took a back seat when I received a bad grade because I could not frame well-formed sentences in (US) English, and it was indicated how glad I should be as I am now part of a well-known urban sociologist's first world coterie of students.

My learning in urban sociology, however, again took a front seat due to the kindness of another urban sociologist who later also became my PhD supervisor. Once my teaching assistantship as part of the PhD came to an end, I started teaching independent courses and urban sociology was a core course that I would teach. This not only gave me a little more control but also took me into conceptual terrains around cities and border crossings, spatial segregations, and racialised hierarchies. Questions such as the connections between cities such as Kolkata and Buffalo, the mapping of cities onto gender, race and caste, the migration histories of social groups, and the spatialised commodity circuits of capital began to concern me that would then become moments for self-reflection and further study.

CONCLUSION **161**

Through the teaching of urban sociology, I gained some confidence in myself as well as in the conceptual field of what I came to later know as social geography. Later through participation in conferences I came into contact with social geographers and then there were collaborations and more learning. So in a way I am in an interloper in the world of social geography but also an avid learner, and in awe of all of your work!

KATH: So my story connects with all of yours, I think. I left Ireland at the age of 18 to do Physical Education (PE) and Sports Science and Geography at Loughborough University in England. It was the first time I had ever been to England and I definitely saw Geography as my second subject, that I needed in order to teach PE in Ireland. I got all the way to my final year and applied for my PGCE (Postgraduate Certificate of Education) which is the secondary school teaching qualification in PE and Geography. In the final term of my final year, I was doing Sarah Holloway's feminist geographies module and a dissertation on women's football in England and the US. Not lesbian geographies, but I was getting closer! I was reading David Bell and Gill Valentine's Mapping Desire and until that point I didn't know Geography could be about sexualities! Sarah told me that Gill Valentine had a new social and cultural geography masters at Sheffield University. It wasn't something that I would have found on my own, or even considered myself to be the 'kind of person' who did a Masters. I was terrified but I thought it was an amazing opportunity and I deferred my PGCE and I went and did my social and cultural geographies masters with Gill Valentine. I loved it, I loved what was open to study and all the subject areas. Then I got a funded PhD in Cheltenham with Cara Aitchison. So, my PhD on Power, Performativity and Place, my start in lesbian/sexualities/queer geographies, was because of feminist and queer geographers who made space for me.

III. MESSY SOCIAL GEOGRAPHIES

KATH: So let us move to recapping key concepts and ideas that are coming through in the book.

162 CONCLUSION

DHIREN: I presume when we started thinking about 'messy' social geographies, we wanted to distance ourselves from the way in which conventional social geography textbooks were written. Most of these wanted to provide a very neat analysis of both how social spaces are produced and social lives are lived and articulated. *We want to begin by illustrating that our identities and lives are messy, and therefore the ways in which we live our lives are going to produce social relationships which are equally messy.* Conventional modes of knowing that are obsessed with neatness have often asked to surrender and compartmentalise us, or rather fractured us and put us into well-defined identity boxes. We need to understand that these messy social relationships produce messy geographies. This book is a humble attempt to initiate a dialogue on understanding what these messy geographies look like when we look at the world through an intersectional spatial lens.

KATH: That's a lovely way of putting it.

NIHARIKA: So, some of the key concepts that we worked with in this book were *space* and *time*. When I think of these two key concepts that hold social geography together, I would ask the reader to think about these as non-linear and in that sense, messy. Social relations do not fall into neat territorial boxes. Therefore concepts such as space and time cannot be neatly arranged and must be flexible enough to explain messy social relations. So, messy means non-linear. By messy we also mean complex axes of power that cannot always be understood in a straightforward fashion. So for instance, when I talked about my anxieties in Buffalo, I was definitely at the receiving end of my teacher's perceptions about me, who was a white older male and was from the first world. At the same time, considering my own geographical context, I have taken birth in a high caste family of doctors and lawyers which has equipped me with cultural capital to cross over into the United States as a graduate student.

KATH: I agree, and for me the key concepts that we need to emphasise are *power, inequality, justice, difference* and that messiness isn't experienced in the same way by everyone, everywhere. For me, difference isn't just about exclusion and marginalisation. It can also be about resistance, celebration, happiness, protest, and creating social change – those kind of aspects as well.

CONCLUSION **163**

DHIREN: I was thinking about two things. One, the foundational concepts within human geography, and the other, about this prefix of social and what does it add to them. For instance, if you're thinking about *distance* as a conceptual tool, what does it mean when you say social distance? But also think about what constitutes this 'social' when we are writing/discussing it. The way in which the discipline has grown and been obsessed with neatness is also a negotiation of this boundary making. Who is (kept) inside and outside academia? Who do we write about in our journal articles? What are the modes through which we classify and categorise us and them to perpetuate a specific ordering of society? So one way we want to think is about who wants to make sure that it stays in neat compartments. Which institutions have and hold power in this regard? And in the times of speaking about *decolonising knowledge*, is the picture changing? Does this usage of messiness actually allow us to question that epistemological neatness that's strong within the structure of knowledge production?

Even with these key concepts of *social distance/location/space and time* that are probably foundational in human geography and we teach at undergrad level, what does social as a prefix do? Like what does it mean to women stepping out late at night exploring, loitering, working in urban social spaces which are deeply gendered and recruit violence to exclude them? What does social distance mean for trans women sex workers soliciting on streets amidst police surveillance and the violent city? And what does their interaction and co-occupancy of spaces with middle-class women from respectable families tell us about geographies of morality and contested claiming of spaces? In another account, what does social distance mean as a language that was being circulated during the COVID-19 pandemic? Public health departments and governments had asked us to maintain a certain degree of social distance to combat the spread of virus. But how does it spatially articulate where communities are already placed in relation to each other in certain distances through social-spatial segregation based on caste, religion, race, and so on? Aren't we already familiar with ghettos and hoods and *bastis*[2] in India? In an already heightened communal climate, certain Muslim dominated neighbourhoods came to be classified as COVID-19

164 CONCLUSION

hotspots in Delhi. What does this creation of distance serve to save us from the virus and also how do already segregated communities get to be labelled as both contagion and the virus? In another instance, a respectable middle-class neighbourhood built a wall to separate themselves from the predominantly Dalit *basti* in South Delhi and to save themselves from the virus by exaggerating the existing physical and social distance between the two settlements. In this process, compartmentalising them and closing the only way out for the people in the *basti*. To speak of messiness in geographies is to then understand these complex layerings and mappings.

MARY: It's interesting that we have similarities and differences in what we think are the important concepts, and how we make sense of social geography. For me, I think the key concepts are *distance, time, space and place; power; movement; difference*; and something that's like connections or networks or relations.

KATH: Would you put *communities* in there as well, in that kind of umbrella, or would that not be separate?

MARY: I think that that would fall under my sense of relations because I see that communities matter, but the naming of a community creates a boundary that is not quite how people live. So that's why I'd focus on the relationships and the connections that take a variety of different forms, but I am not an assemblage thinker. Like I think assemblages probably matter like they've mattered in how people have been practising social geography and geography, more generally, over the last while but I don't find the concept that useful. So I think we need to acknowledge it, but I don't think it's a key concept. Okay that's enough from me.

NIHARIKA: In sociology, community has been a key concept, along with group. Sociology has typically followed a conventional understanding of communities and groups, which talks about familiarity and likeness between the people who make up communities and groups; this has a spatial and temporal aspect as well. Differences within are not much the focus of attention in the discipline as much as difference between. This is because sociology's core concern has been the question of social order and what maintains it despite societal upheavals. If one were to engage with the concept of community via this book, then

CONCLUSION **165**

the question of familiarity as it relates to the condition of social order will be under question. The role of a community may not necessarily be to maintain social order, but also to question it. When community becomes a refuge for marginalised persons, then it may become a launchpad for upending social order, as we saw in the chapter on protests and activisms. So, I'm just trying to bring some complexity to community here; where familiarity and difference work together to question those place-specific structures that hierarchise on the basis of difference and work to maintain them. I do think there is a value in thinking beyond community. But at the same time, if one thinks of communities of protest as we saw in Chapter 1 and in Chapter 3, then we are working with considerations of power, inequality and marginalisation. This is how we may conceptually mess up the boundaries of community.

KATH: I think it's a nice play at those boundaries of the messiness. And this book is really at the messy intersection of geographies and social life as it is broadly conceived across the social sciences. I think that's why it's not just written by social geographers, it's also that you (Niharika) are a key author in this as well. I think that's really useful to think about those multiple ways of thinking through communities and that as a key concept for you.

MARY: I also think that social geography has been obsessed with *the urban and cities* and that's an obsession that continues today and is mirrored more broadly in geography, with its emphasis on the planetary urban. And that is also a problem because of the creation of separations between urban and rural, between what is seen as advanced or more civilised or a space of encounter or interaction, rather than recognising the co-dependence of different spaces and different groups of people on each other.

One important thing that I completely forgot to mention earlier is *scale*. I think that social geography offers a really interesting site for exploring scale, especially the relationships between different scales like the 'local' and the 'global'. This scalar relationship is also not to be understood as stable, but can vary so that there could be local within the global and vice versa, depending on hierarchical access to resources and opportunities.

166 CONCLUSION

DHIREN: Because the focus is also around the transformative power of social justice, I was also thinking about concepts like *social transformation* and how it manifests in *spatial transformation* and vice versa. Or social change and spatial change. And if we could also bring those things to engage with challenges to think about what social change is in the first place. As geographers we are trying to say how social changes are also inherently spatial in character, that it formulates and shapes spatial relations and lots of variations of power that manifest.

MARY: If we are interested in spatial transformation, we need to be able to tell the story of social geography in many different ways, including quantitative. Quantitative measures can be very helpful if they're being used to try and communicate alternatives, rather than to confirm a particular kind of reality, if that makes sense. So, I think numbers are very powerful for social geographers but it's about using them in a liberatory way rather than in a reinforcing way. So I think social geographies need quantitative tools. And I think that cartography is also a really powerful tool for social geographers. But it's about being able to deconstruct the map and to reconstruct the map, rather than taking the map as truth. And I think the map as truth is a particular challenge at the moment because of the ubiquity of digital cartography technologies. We all live with maps, but we don't think about what they mean in quite the same way, so I think we need those skills also.

I think the key tool that a social geographer needs is to recognise that there always is an alternative. I'm not sure if hope is a tool, or an outlook, but a social geographer has to be hopeful that things can change. So rather than getting caught up in that form of social or environmental determinism that has marked an awful lot of social geography in the past, it's the recognition of what's changed, whether that change comes from political activism or from encounters, whether it's collective or individual. Change is always place-based in some form, and it is about changing place and our relationship with place and space too.

DHIREN: However, often such number games seem fatal for communities that cannot afford to be too visible and countable or

CONCLUSION 167

who are likely to be peripheralised and called miniscule minorities. In 2013 when the Supreme Court of India reinstated the sodomy law, the judges asked the courtroom if they knew any gays as he himself did not. Though the court was full of queer lawyers and activists, none could stand and mark their presence. The judges went ahead and reinstated the colonial-era section 377 of Indian Penal Code stating that we are dealing with a miniscule minority.

But, I do agree with Mary here to a degree, that these numbers often help to speak to regimes of power and ask for change. For example, to speak of the number of homeless and poor people below the poverty line to seek policy interventions. Or how many people died during the pandemic due to lack of medical care and state support. However, many times this data is also manufactured by the state in how it intends to read and make certain persons legible and recognised as citizen subjects. The official data then already premises through ways in which social realities are understood and recognised by power. Independent researchers often try to counter such narratives by producing their own sets of data like the fact finding reports we do. Like sometimes we need to mobilise numbers to be seen and heard in the form of protests and resistance.

KATH: I agree with you both that the notion of change and the idea of hope is key. Hopelessness that can be kind of the end point of critical discussions of power. So, for me, what is key is not just talking about how things are awful but also talking about how things can change and people are empowered to do that.

IV. BOUNDARIES OF SOCIAL GEOGRAPHY

KATH: Coming back to Dhiren's question about the social and the boundaries of the social as a prefix to Geographies, messiness can challenge those boundaries and it can feel like social geographies is a mishmash of everything and therefore nothing. The question that I am constantly asked by students 'Why are we doing this? Is it a waste of time? Do we need social geographies? We've got sociology, why do we need social geographies?'

168 CONCLUSION

MARY: Yeah and I think that the two key concepts are the social and the geography. So we're starting from there and it's pretty obvious that no one really agrees what either of those mean. We've been writing about social geography but recognising that the boundaries of social geography are both constructed and also deeply unclear. And so it raises lots of questions about what exactly social geography is; how exactly social geography works; the amount of labour that goes into differentiating social geography from other kinds of geography when actually at its core it's about the relationship between people and place with each of those broadly defined.

When I was writing the introduction, it felt like I had no idea what that was. So, one of the things that struck me about trying to pull this book together is that there are key concepts that work through geography as a whole. How we understand them within social geography is a process of differentiation and a set of ideas that actually don't really serve to ask the bigger questions about why lives are the way they are; what gives rise to those lives; and what is restricted because of the ways in which lives are lived in different places? So in a way, I think we can go back to very simple and straightforward concepts in thinking through social geography. What makes them messy is people who, in all of the various ways in which they organise themselves, create the kinds of distinctions and differentiation that lead to the messiness. And I'm saying people, but it's also about more than people so that's been another realisation: that the social is not just about social relations between humans, but it's also the social more broadly defined.

DHIREN: Probably also to geographically think about what/where social geography is. For instance in India, there are not many geography departments. And there are fewer departments where social geography is taught. It would be interesting to map how, across different regions, social feeds the discipline itself. This division is articulated when we talk about European geographies and American geographies or what happens when we think about Africa, or how it is understood at the level of individual university departments.

CONCLUSION **169**

KATH: You said the boundaries of social geography are unclear, because they're unclear within geography. Would you also agree that there's something unclear about the social aspect of that in the boundaries between, say, social geography and sociology or social sciences, more broadly? That kind of almost creating those boundaries, by seeking to say 'Oh, this is social geography', may be more problematic when actually the main thing is to explore why lives are the way they are, what else they might be?

MARY: Yeah, there are lots of different kinds of messiness, but one of them is precisely about the way that academic disciplines have developed with their insistence on differentiation and hierarchies. The kinds of processes we're talking about in the book are also the kinds of processes that work in the creation of knowledge and through the academy. So the further subdivision of a discipline like geography, the creation of distinctions and differentiation between social geography or geography and sociology or social science or social policy, that desperate need to bound and delineate and define is, I suppose, an attempt to counter the messiness, but it's also a futile exercise, other than an exercise in the assertion of academic and disciplinary power.

KATH: I think naming social geography continues to be important. Even as we might claim, and I would agree, that its boundaries are fluid, porous, not clearly defined and shouldn't be. But I think naming social geography does something both within geography but also outside of geography within kind of broader social sciences, that is important. So within geography, I think it needs to said that social lives are key and for me social geographies bring us that to the forefront. I also think within sociology, social policy, social work, and the broader social sciences naming the spatial as more than just a container offers important geographical insights in these areas.

That might be unfair for a lot of the more recent work in these areas. Maybe space is more than a container, but equally I think there's something crucial about the way that geographers look at the social. We see that place matters but also places are constitutive of social, and that still remains distinct. So, I think it's a distinct lens, or maybe a distinct set of tools. I don't think it's about having an

170 CONCLUSION

amorphous mass called social science and not necessarily naming the ways we see, and how we create knowledge. So while I agree with you, Mary, I also would see the importance of naming social geographies and thinking about the spatial as crucial, even as we might question its boundaries.

NIHARIKA: Yes, Kath, but when creating the boundaries, I am thinking about the 'insider/outsider' question as well. So, what does it mean to be an 'outsider in the discipline'? This question itself points towards the condition that there are disciplinary boundaries between sociology and social geography. So in a sociological theory undergraduate class concepts such as modernity, industrialisation, capitalism are key. While space and time are referred to, they are not the primary focus. Can I say that if space and time were the primary focus through which we learn about modernity, then we would enter the field of social geography? Again, in an introduction to sociology class, when we teach class, race, caste, gender, sexuality, and so on, concepts such as space and time are not upfront, but would be in a social geography class. So, as someone trained in sociology, I do think that social geography has distinguishing markers. Further, what if we were to (as sociologists teaching an undergraduate class) think about social change, a key concept in sociology, in spatial and temporal terms? Would we be trying to understand change in order to see how it functions to maintain order or would we push students to think about how place, space, and scale has a potential for transformation (and not just change). I do think social geography and sociology can be put to radical use through their interdisciplinary conversations.

V. THINKING FOR NEW FUTURES

KATH: We've discussed our journeys, messiness, and boundaries of social geographies, now we turn to thinking about hopeful futures and some of the ways (tools) we might think of them.

MARY: I think social geographies could make a really important future contribution by focusing on how power works more broadly. I think there's been too much of an emphasis on marginal groups and marginal spaces throughout the history of

CONCLUSION 171

what we might distinguish as social geography. That emphasis on groups with less power, or on groups who are isolated or marginalised or separate, draws attention away from the broader issue of how power works. And how it works to separate and segregate and maintain privilege for small groups of people.

DHIREN: Geographers often write about marginality and people as framed into narratives of victimisation as a geographical or sociological text. What if we were to say such imagination needs to be reframed. Rather than having this saviour mentality, a distance that perpetuates the status quo, we need to learn not impose a singular narrative over everyone and cultivate reflexivity. Chapter 1 starts with a poem written by a Dalit woman. Although a translation, but originally written in a language which is not what academy speaks in. It talks about reversing the gaze and subverting power. It questions what is considered centre and what is usually mapped as periphery and margin. What if we turn it around? The poet says how structures claim us as the far end, at the boundary, at the fringe. Rather, I am the Centre and you will have to listen to me. For the village does not end at my house but it starts from where we live. Social spaces are transforming and it's because their homogeneity has been disrupted. The gates that were very meticulously maintained have been thrashed open and people are moving in. Bringing specifics of their sociality, historicity, and spatiality, which is then turning the narrative upside down. What happens if and when we speak – we bust myths, write ourselves into histories, of our doings, of our resistance, of our victories. That's something that probably as we are writing this book, we are trying to do. To speak of hope as social geography, not just as geographies of despair.

KATH: I think that's really amazing and really resonates for me around that kind of geographies of victimisation rather than necessarily marginal geographies. I like it, because it's the victimisation that leads to hopelessness, but also the saviour complex that people can take up when reading from particular places (perhaps Global North, perhaps urban centres) about these populations. Their desire to 'save' and rescue and fix 'other places' can come from a place of wanting to make things better, wanting to do something, but so often it can fail to see the 'here and

CONCLUSION

now', their own power relations and complicities in the injustices being created. The desire to see 'something being done' is a valuable motivator, and need to engage with power relations in ways that create genuine change – even if that change seems small.

DHIREN: A point that I wanted to add here as we question the geographers' obsession with writing of/about marginalisation and marginalised people, and often, that is the reason why a lot of us and students get into this saviour complex mode. With decline in public funding in education in India that facilitated a much diverse cohort in the classroom, we are witnessing amidst neoliberalisation of education, a proliferation of expensive private universities in various places. This would imply that the book we are writing as an introductory text in social geography might be engaged with by more and more privileged students and less and less of people from the margins. This becomes necessary then, for us, to imagine social geographies from our own social contexts. And think of that through relations of power and to not just think about it like studying some cool Black neighbourhood which is mapped as the centre of crime in our city. So while teaching at an Indian university, we tend to tell people why we don't write about our caste geographies, like the majority of students and their upper-caste position and how it produces a particular set of social relations and exclusions. That, rather than writing about people that need to be saved, let's turn that gaze around towards us.

KATH: I think there can also be a feeling of 'I'm really privileged, I can't possibly do anything, I'll just be in the saviour complex' and that can be paralysing. Or hierarchies of oppression: I'm oppressed this way but I'm not oppressed enough so therefore I shouldn't really do anything.

DHIREN: A lot of my students also stare at me saying 'Oh! are you like targeting me?'.

We need to stop looking at it as an attack on us but the system that is being kept in place to organise power in particular ways, which affords us a privileged position. What possibilities can this acknowledgement or inward looking allow us? Probably building solidarity networks? To rethink our relationship with the communities that

CONCLUSION **173**

we are working and surrounded with. And not just this saviour/ victim paradigm that we are used to. Because it's an easy paradigm and it's an easy framework to work, right. What does it mean, then, to be an ally? What kind of social geographies does that produce?

KATH: That nicely swings us back to the messy social geographies because there are no easy answers, or solutions. Asking for something contextual is about us as well, and not just shouting at or protesting 'them' 'over there'.

What are some of the 'tools' we could think of, or offer to readers though?

NIHARIKA: I think one of the tools is to get to know the place that one lives in and even though this is a cliché it can be a useful entry point. How does one get to know the place that one lives in? To go about this, one can look at:

- A census and when was the first census done
- A map and who has made that map
- City/municipal records to get to know what are the infrastructure, neighbourhood distribution of population and such
- Talking to people in the place that one is familiar with and asking them where would they not live, or not go, and why

So, this is a very basic way to get to know the geography of a place. As you check this, ask yourself:

- Who are the people that stay there? Do they look like me?
- Are they like me, or are they different from me?
- Who are the people who are different from me and where do they stay?

Related to this, you can ask yourself:

- Who is living in what place in that town or city or village where you are living?
- Who is living with who?
- Who is similar to me and who is different from me?

So that would be a very easy way to get into kind of a social geographical mapping of the city (or the place you live?). This mapping is different from the one that a cartographer has made or an urban planner. The person who is reading this book can come up with a map them-/her-/himself and compare it with one that has been made by a cartographer or a planner and see what emerges from this comparison.

KATH: I think that's really interesting and for me, it's difficult to think of in terms of tools. But if I was to offer tools, it would be it moving on from the map, it would be about considering:

- Who can be in those places that you go to regularly, like shopping, socialising, working?
- Who can't and in what ways?
- Do you move through places easily, like airports? What passport do you have, what access does it give you?
- Where am I welcome/unwelcome? What ways do I 'know' this?
- Where am I nervous/on guard?
- Who doesn't have to be worried about places they go? And that even that feeling of 'I can go anywhere', what does that tell you about the places you go? About who you are?

Then, for me when I feel welcome and part of a place, I think 'oh I'll just help others'. In one piece of research early in my career, I thought community/participatory research was about 'helping them'. I soon learned that I had more to learn from them. It was a real kind of eye opener for how researchers and people who've been to university can occupy these privileged positions, but where 'helping' is actually disempowering. What's needed are the tools you can bring, the access you can give to particular spaces or corridors of power, but you also need to listen and to learn. So as a tool, I think knowing where you can and should listen and learn from those who don't occupy space like you do is really important. And on the other hand, realising that you aren't 'helping': you are working together as an ally and you get a lot out of it too.

DHIREN: I was thinking why place is very important, so also thinking of the feeling of placelessness that one often feels. And that's

CONCLUSION **175**

where we are. We are trying to find a place for ourselves. Like often we are arbitrarily told within the corridors of the discipline, that what we do or study is not geography. One then needs to stop and ask, what is geography, and where is geography? How is geography enabling us to think about, say, social sexual political lives?

In the department where I studied we were obsessed with quantitative research. I think that most of the people then who are/were involved in studying social inequality would say let's do disparity index, let's map social inequality on the map. I feel extremely uncomfortable with this framework of reducing people into numbers. Translating a full complex person into a number, which can then be flattened out and put next to another number and clubbed together to create a particular kind of data to be represented into a pattern. And you're nothing more than empirics for a researcher from an urban centre and privileged location who goes to marginalised locations and communities, because academia historically has been obsessed with poverty porn. We go there to look for data, and then the data we are looking for are often numbers; and I'm saying that for people like the prisoners and people who are now entering the university, we are challenging it and stating that we are more than just numbers, but are messy stories. One of the tools for me then, in terms of social geographic knowledge is this spatial storytelling. But to also acknowledge what kind of stories are brought into our classrooms, that narrate our lives? What are these stories and how are these stories about places and connections and networks of people? And how can we think through them? I use the following ways to engage and map, this may be useful for others too.

1   We start with drawing a map of the city most are familiar with (or a hypothetical city) and ask them to locate two or three places they feel very safe in, and similarly places they feel unsafe at. Given the diversity of the classroom, how that becomes a contested site when you have called somebody else's home an unsafe space. What do these contestations reveal about their social geographies?

2   The other thing we do is to go to the city and walk with other people and see the city from their vantage point. When you're walking with the person, what do you get to know about the city, both in and also about yourself when you're doing that spatial negotiation? Like, for instance, if you're walking with a gender non-conforming trans friend of yours and you're walking in the city of Delhi, where the city already wants to read the Trans person as sex worker, are you ready to risk your comfortable distance of researcher and researched and allow yourself to be seen differently by the city? If she is seen as a sex worker, what is the city reading you as?

> MARY: It's always interesting to talk after others have spoken because it shifts and changes what I think I want to say. I really liked Dhiren's description of social geographies as telling spatial stories. I think the key tool that a social geographer needs is curiosity. So, to be curious about the world that they live in and to recognise that their experience is not a universal truth. That's the starting point for telling spatial stories.

VI. CONCLUSION

We enjoyed these conversations and we hope that these discussions open up considerations of yourselves, your lives, and the challenges we face. The reason we're doing this book is with a hope that change is possible. We are hopeful that people who read this book will engage with social lives, their own, and everybody else's, in more diverse ways, rather than the constrained ways in which our social vision is conditionally constructed. There are no right answers or definitive solutions or actions. Instead, the potential lies in, and with, us and along with others who are 'not like us'.

NOTES

1 We wrote this chapter by first recording a series of three conversations between us over Zoom. Kath then edited these transcripts into a document and created the headings. The transcript itself was a testament to power relations where some of our voices/names/terms were much more easily and

CONCLUSION **177**

correctly interpreted by the automatic transcription software (those of us from Ireland) than others (those of us from India). As each of us edited our own words, before looking at each other's, the labour was inequitably distributed towards those of us whose voices are not as recognizable and heard by transcription.

2 *Basti* is used to indicate a slum area in the city.

REFERENCES

Adey, P. *Mobility*. 2nd ed. London & New York: Routledge, 2017.

Ahmed, A. *Social Geography*. New Delhi: Rawat Books, 1999.

Akinwotu, E. and W. Strzyżyńska. "Nigeria condemns treatment of Africans trying to flee Ukraine." *The Guardian*, 28 February 2022.

Ali, H. A. *Introduction to the Social Geography of India: Concepts, Problems, and Prospects*. London: Routledge, 2023.

Antonsich, M. "Searching for belonging – An analytical framework." *Geography Compass* 4, no. 6 (2010): 644–659. https://doi.org/10.1111/j.1749-8198.2009.00317.x

Archana, K. C. "Life of dignity: India's first state-backed Dairy Farm provides livelihood to transgenders." *IndiaTimes*, 28 October 2020.

Babar, Z., M. Ewers and N. Khattab. "Im/mobile highly skilled migrants in Qatar." *Journal of Ethnic and Migration Studies* 45, no. 9 (2019): 1553–1570. https://doi.org/10.1080/1369183X.2018.1492372

Banerjea, N. and K. Browne. *Liveable Lives*. London: Bloomsbury, 2023.

Berg, L. D. "Scaling knowledge: Towards a critical geography of critical geographies." *Geoforum* 35, no. 5 (2004): 553–558. https://doi.org/10.1016/j.geoforum.2004.01.005.

Berg, L. D., U. Best, M. Gilmartin and H. Gutzon Larsen, eds. *Placing Critical Geography*. London & New York: Routledge, 2022.

Bhowmick, N. "'I cannot be intimated. I cannot be bought'. The women leading India's farmers protests." *Time*, 4 March 2021.

Blunt, A. and J. Wills. *Dissident Geographies: An Introduction to Radical Ideas and Practice*. Harlow: Longman, 2000.

Borde, R. and B. Bluemling. "Representing indigenous sacred land: The case of the Niyamgiri movement in India." *Capitalism Nature Socialism* 32, no. 1 (2021): 68–87. https://doi.org/10.1080/10455752.2020.1730417

Bunge, W. *Fitzgerald: Geography of a Revolution*. Athens, GA: University of Georgia Press, 2011.

REFERENCES **179**

Butler, J. "Can one lead a good life in a bad life?" *Radical Philosophy* 176 (2012): 9–18.

Butler, J. *Frames of War: When Is Life Grievable?* London: Verso, 2010.

Buttimer, A. (1968) "Social geography". In *International Encyclopedia of the Social Sciences*. The Macmillan Company and the Free Press. Available online at https://researchrepository.ucd.ie/bitstream/10197/10722/1/SocialGeography.pdf

Castillo, R. "Feeling at home in the 'Chocolate City': An exploration of place-making practices and structures of belonging amongst Africans in Guangzhou." *Inter-Asia Cultural Studies* 15, no. 2 (2014): 235–257. https://doi.org/10.1080/14649373.2014.911513

Chan, K. W. "Internal migration in China: Integrating migration with Urbanization policies and Hokou reform." *KNOMAD Policy Brief 16*, November 2021. https://www.knomad.org/publication/internal-migration-china-integrating-migration-urbanization-policies-and-hukou-reform

Country, B., S. Wright, S. Suchet-Pearson et al. "Co-becoming Bawaka: Towards a relational understanding of place/space." *Progress in Human Geography* 40, no. 4 (2016): 455–475. https://doi.org/10.1177/0309132515589437

Crang, M. and J. Zhang. "Transient dwelling: Trains as places of identification for the floating population of China." *Social & Cultural Geography* 13, no. 8 (2012): 895–914. https://doi.org/10.1080/14649365.2012.728617

Crenshaw, K. "Mapping the margins: Intersectionality, identity politics, and violence against women of color." *Stanford Law Review* 43, no. 6 (1991): 12–41.

Cresswell, T. *In Place/Out of Place: Geography, Ideology, and Transgression*. Minneapolis, MN: University of Minnesota Press, 1996.

Cresswell, T. "Towards a politics of mobility." *Environment and Planning D: Society and Space* 28 (2010): 17–31.

Datta, A. "The 'Smart safe city': Gendered Time, speed, and violence in the margins of India's urban age." *Annals of the American Association of Geographers* 110, no. 5 (2020): 1318–1334.

Del Casino, V. J. *Social Geography: A Critical Introduction*. Oxford: Wiley-Blackwell, 2009.

Del Casino, V. J., M. E. Thomas, P. Cloke and R. Panelli, eds. *A Companion to Social Geography*. Oxford: Wiley-Blackwell, 2011.

Della Porta, D., A. Lavizzari and H. Reiter. "The spreading of the Black Lives Matter movement campaign: The Italian case in cross-national perspective." *Sociological Forum* 37, no. 3 (2022): 700–721. https://doi.org/10.1111/socf.12818

Dunbar, G. S. "Some early occurrences of the term 'social geography'." *Scottish Geographical Magazine* 93, no. 1 (1977): 15–20. https://doi.org/10.1080/00369227708736353

Dutta, A. "Contradictory tendencies: The Supreme Court's NALSA judgment on transgender recognition and rights." *Journal of Indian Law and Society* 5, Monsoon (2014): 225–236.

180 REFERENCES

Esson, J., P. Noxolo, R. Baxter, P. Daley and M. Byron. "The 2017 RGS-IBG chair's theme: Decolonising geographical knowledges, or reproducing coloniality?" *Area* 49, no. 3 (2017): 384–388. https://doi.org/10.1111/area.12371

Evans, B., S. Bias and R. Colls. "The dys-appearing fat body: Bodily intensities and fatphobic sociomaterialities when flying while fat." *Annals of the American Association of Geographers* 111, no. 6 (2021): 1816–1832. https://doi.org/10.1080/24694452.2020.1866485

Gardner, A., S. Pessoa, A. Diop, K. Al-Ghanim, K. Le Trung and L. Harkness. "A portrait of low-income migrants in contemporary Qatar." *Journal of Arabian Studies* 3, no. 1 (2013): 1–17. https://doi.org/10.1080/21534764.2013.806076

Gillespie, K. and R.-C. Collard. *Critical Animal Geographies: Politics, Intersections, and Hierarchies in a Multispecies World*. London and New York: Routledge, 2017.

Gilmartin, M., P. Burke Wood and C. O'Callaghan. *Borders, Mobility and Belonging*. London: Policy Press, 2018.

Graham, M. and M. Amir Anwar. "The global gig economy: Towards a planetary labour market?" *First Monday* 24, no. 4 (2019). https://doi.org/10.5210/fm.v24i4.9913

Grant, J. and L. Mittelsteadt. "Types of gated communities." *Environment and Planning B: Planning and Design* 31, no. 6 (2004): 913–930. https://doi.org/10.1068/b3165

Hall, E. and E. Bates. "Hatescape? A relational geography of disability hate crime, exclusion and belonging in the city." *Geoforum* 101 (2019): 100–110. https://doi.org/10.1016/j.geoforum.2019.02.024

Harris, E. and M. Nowicki. Cultural geographies of precarity. *Cultural Geographies* 25, no. 3 (2018): 387–391. https://doi.org/10.1177/1474474018762812

Harvey, D. *Social Justice and the City*. Revised ed. Athens GA: University of Georgia Press, 2009.

Hladchenko, M. "International students in Ukraine: A gateway to developed countries." *European Journal of Higher Education*. Published online: 22 October 2021. https://doi.org/10.1080/21568235.2021.1988669

Ho, E. L.-E. "African student migrants in China: Negotiating the global geographies of power through gastronomic practices and culture." *Food, Culture & Society* 21, no. 1 (2018): 9–24. https://doi.org/10.1080/15528014.2017.1398468

Ho, E. L.-E. "Social geography II: Space and sociality." *Progress in Human Geography* 6, no. 5 (2022): 1252–1260. https://doi.org/10.1177/03091325221103601

Houghteling, C. and P. A. Dantzler. "Taking a knee, taking a stand: Social networks and identity salience in the 2017 NFL protests." *Sociology of Race and Ethnicity* 6, no. 3 (2020): 396–415. https://doi.org/10.1177/2332649219885978

Imrie, R. "Disability and discourses of mobility and movement." *Environment and Planning A* 32, no. 9 (2000): 1641–1656.

Jarrett, K. *Digital Labor*. Cambridge and Medford, MA: Policy Press, 2022.

REFERENCES 181

John, M. E. "Intersectionality: Rejection or critical dialogue?" *Economic and Political Weekly* 50, no. 33 (2015): 72–76.

Jones, E. and J. Eyles. *An Introduction to Social Geography.* Oxford: Oxford University Press, 1979.

Jones, J. P. III, H. Leitner, S. A. Marston and E. Sheppard. "Neil Smith's scale." *Antipode* 49, no. 1 (2017): 138–152.

Jones, R. *Violent Borders: Refugees and the Right to Move.* London: Verso, 2016.

Kitchin, R. M., D. Jacobson, R. G. Golledge and M. Blades. "Belfast without sight: Exploring geographies of blindness." *Irish Geography* 31, no. 1 (1998): 34–46. https://doi.org/10.1080/00750779809478630

Kostenwein, D. "Between walls and fences: How different types of gated communities shape the streets around them." *Urban Studies* 58, no. 16 (2021): 3230–3246. https://doi.org/10.1177%2F0042098020984320

Lefebvre, H. *The Production of Space* (trans. Donald Nicholson-Smith). Malden, MA and Oxford: Blackwell, 1991.

Leib, J. I. "Separate times, shared spaces: Arthur Ashe, Monument Avenue and the politics of Richmond, Virginia's symbolic landscape." *Cultural Geographies* 9, no. 3 (2002): 286–312. https://doi.org/10.1191/1474474002eu250oa

Liang, K. and P. Le Billon. "African migrants in China: Space, race and embodied encounters in Guangzhou, China." *Social & Cultural Geography* 21, no. 5 (2020): 602–628. https://doi.org/10.1080/14649365.2018.1514647

Livingstone, D. *The Geographical Tradition.* Malden, MA and Oxford: Blackwell, 1992.

Magris, C. *Microcosms* (trans. I. Halliday). London: The Harvill Press, 1999.

Massey, D. *For Space.* London, New Delhi and Thousand Oaks, CA: Sage, 2005.

Mbembe, A. *Necropolitics* (trans. S. Corcoran). Durham and London: Duke University Press, 2019.

Mbembe, A. "Necropolitics." *Public Culture* 15, no. 1 (2003): 11–40. https://doi.org/10.1215/08992363-15-1-11

Menon, N. "Is feminism about 'women'? A critical view on intersectionality from India." *Economic and Political Weekly* 50, no. 17 (2015): 37–44.

Merriman, P. "Human geography without time-space." *Transactions of the Institute of British Geographers* 37, no. 1 (2011): 13–27.

Mitchell, K., R. Jones and J. Fluri, eds. *Handbook on Critical Geographies of Migration.* Cheltenham: Edward Elgar Publishing, 2019.

Morakabati, Y., J. Beavis and J. Fletcher. "Planning for a Qatar without oil: Tourism and economic diversification, a battle of perceptions." *Tourism Planning & Development* 11, no. 4 (2014): 415–434. https://doi.org/10.1080/21568316.2014.884978s

Mu, X., A. G.-O. Yeh and X. Zhang. "The interplay of spatial spread of COVID-19 and human mobility in the urban system of China during the Chinese New Year." *Environment and Planning B: Urban Analytics and City Science* 48, no. 7 (2021): 1955–1971. https://doi.org/10.1177/2399808320954211

REFERENCES

Ness, I., ed. *The Routledge Handbook of the Gig Economy*. London and New York: Routledge, 2022.

Newcastle Social Geographies Collective. *Social Geographies: An Introduction*. Lanham, MD: Rowman & Littlefield, 2021.

Pain, R., J. Gough, G. Mowl, M. Barke, R. MacFarlene and D. Fuller. *Introducing Social Geographies*. London and New York: Routledge, 2001.

Panelli, R. *Social Geographies: From Difference to Action*. London: Sage, 2004.

Parsons, M. "Governing with care, reciprocity, and relationality: Recognising the connectivity of human and more-than-human wellbeing and the process of decolonization." *Dialogues in Human Geography* 13, no. 2 (2023): 288–292. https://doi.org/10.1177/20438206221144819

Pattisson, P. et al. "Revealed: 6,500 migrant workers have died in Qatar since World Cup awarded." *The Guardian*, 23 February 2021.

Peet, R. *Modern Geographical Thought*. Malden, MA and Oxford: Blackwell Publishing, 1998.

Pratt, G. *Families Apart: Migrant Mothers and the Conflicts of Labour and Love*. Minneapolis, MN: University of Minnesota Press, 2012.

Raju, S. "We Are Different, But Can We Talk?" *Gender, Place and Culture: A Journal of Feminist Geography* 9, no. 2 (2002): 173–177.

Raju, S., M. S. Kumar and S. Corbridge, eds. *Colonial and Post-Colonial Geographies of India*. New Delhi: Sage, 2006.

Raza, M. *A Survey of Research in Geography 1969–72*. Bombay: Allied, 1979.

Richardson, D., N. Castree, M. F. Goodchild, A. Kobayashi, W. Liu and R. A. Marston, eds. *The International Encyclopedia of Geography*. Oxford: John Wiley & Sons, 2017. https://doi.org/10.1002/9781118786352.wbieg0874

Rogers, A., N. Castree and R. Kitchin, eds. *A Dictionary of Human Geography*. Oxford: Oxford University Press, 2013.

Routledge, P. *Space Invaders: Radical Geographies of Protest*. London: Pluto Press, 2017.

Routledge, P. and A. Cumbers. *Global Justice Networks: Geographies of Transnational Solidarity*. Manchester: Manchester University Press, 2009.

Said, E. W. *Orientalism*. New York: Vintage Books, 1978.

Samers, M. and M. Collyer. *Migration*. 2nd ed. London and New York: Routledge, 2017.

Seshan, G. "Migrants in Qatar: A socio-economic profile." *Journal of Arabian Studies* 2, no. 2 (2012): 157–171. https://doi.org/10.1080/21534764.2012.735458

Sheller, M. "Theorising mobility justice." *Tempo Social* 30, no. 2 (2018): 17–34.

Simmonds, N., T. Kukutai and J. Rykes. "Here to stay: Reshaping the regions through mana Māori". In P. Spoonley (ed.), *Rebooting the Regions: Why Low or Zero Growth Needn't Mean the End of Prosperity* (pp. 79–105). Wellington: Massey University Press, 2016.

Smith, N. "Marxism and geography in the anglophone world." *Geografische Revue* 3, no. 2 (2001).

Smith, S. J., R. Pain, S. A. Marston and J. P. Jones III, eds. *The Sage Handbook of Social Geographies*. Los Angeles, CA and London: Sage, 2010.

Soundararajan, T. *Trauma of Caste: A Dalit Feminist Meditation on Survivorship, Healing, and Abolition*. New York: North Atlantic Books, 2022.

Steinberg, P. "Blue planet, Black lives: Matter, memory, and the temporalities of political geography." *Political Geography* 96 (2022). https://doi.org/10.1016/j.polgeo.2021.102524

Suda, K. "A room of one's own: Highly educated migrants' strategies for creating a *home* in Guangzhou." *Population, Space and Place* 22, no. 2 (2016): 146–157. https://doi.org/10.1002/psp.1898

Sullivan, C. "Majesty in the city: Experiences of an Aboriginal transgender sex worker in Sydney, Australia". *Gender, Place and Culture* 25, no. 12 (2018): 1681–1702.

Sullivan, J. and J. Cheng. "Contextualising Chinese migration to Africa." *Journal of Asian and African Studies* 53, no. 8 (2018): 1173–1187. https://doi.org/10.1177/0021909618776443

Taylor, K.-Y. *From #BlackLivesMatter to Black Liberation*. Chicago: Haymarket Books, 2016.

Thiong'o, Ngũgĩ wa. *Decolonising the Mind: The Politics of Language in African Literature*. Woodbridge, Suffolk: Boydell & Brewer Ltd, 1986.

Valentine, G. *Social Geographies: Space and Society*. Harlow: Prentice Hall, 2001.

Walia, H. *Undoing Border Imperialism*. Oakland, CA: AK Press, 2013.

Weffer, S. E., R. Dominguez-Martinez and R. Jenkins. "Taking a knee." *Contexts* 17, no. 3 (2018): 66–68. https://doi.org/10.1177/1536504218792529

Xu, J. and A. G. O. Yeh. "Guangzhou." *Cities* 20, no. 5 (2003): 361–374.

Ye, J. "Stayers in China's 'hollowed-out' villages: A counter narrative on massive rural-urban migration." *Population, Space and Place* 24, no. 4 (2018): 21–28. https://doi.org/10.1002/psp.2128

INDEX

Note: page numbers in *italics* indicate a figure and page numbers in **bold** indicate a table on the corresponding page.

abortion, Ireland 42–46, *44*, *46*; *see also* activism
Abortion Rights Campaign (ARC) 43
activism 41, 58–60; 'armchair' 53; repeal, in Ireland 42–46, *44*, *46*; trans, in India 118–120; *see also* protests; resistance
actor-network theory 23
Adivasis 36, 38, 40, 41
age-based communities 76
Ahmed, Aijazuddin 3, 159
Anglo-American geographies 13, 73
animal geographies 81–83
anthropogenic climate change 19
anticolonial/decolonial: approach 19; critiques 5; movements 12; thinkers 29
anticolonialism 12
Arab Spring *35*, 35–36
assemblages 22–23
Association of American Geographers (AAG) 12
asylum seekers 143, 145; *see also* refugees

basti 163–164, 177n2
bauxite 36–37, 40
Bawaka Country 18
Begum, Shamima 98

belonging 26, 97; citizenship and, in Denmark 96–98, 101; hierarchies of, in India 101–103
Berg, Lawrence 13
black geographies 14
#BlackLivesMatter 52–59, *54*
Black people 52–53, 55, 57, 78
Black women 64–65
#BlueLivesMatter 57
bodies 63–65, 67; *see also* identities
Bouazizi, Mohamed 36
Brazil 111
built environments 140, 142, 148–149; *see also* disabling environments
Bunge, William 70
Butler, Judith 92, 95, 96, 114
Buttimer, Anne 2, 155

care work 145–148
Canada, LCP 146–147
capitalism 7, 20–21, 41, 66, 170
Celtic Tiger 106–108
Chicago School 6
China: left-behind children 131; migration in 128–134; smart city technology 87, 89
Chocolate City 133
chromonormativity 18
chunyun 131–132, *132*

INDEX 185

circular migration 129–130
Citizenship Amendment Act (CAA) 101–102, 103
citizenship and belonging 96–103, *100*, *102*
colonialism 9–14, 68, 70, 72; types of 10; *see also* anticolonial/decolonial; anticolonialism
Colston, Edward 56
Combahee River Collective 55
community/communities 37, 164–165; Dalits *see* Dalits; farming 48; feminist 45; Dongrias and Kondh 38; Indigenous 37, 39, 41, 69; making social change possible 58–61; marginalized 66, 113–114; Niyamgiri protests 36–41; place and 52; transgender in India 118–120; *see also* gated communities; LGBTQI+ people; online protests; solidarities
corporations *see* globalization of corporations
countertopography 73
COVID-19 pandemic 55, 59, 87, 108, 119, 126–127, *127*, 163–164
Crenshaw, Kimberlé 64–65
Cresswell, Tim 134, 139
Criminal Tribes Act of 1871 118
crip time 18–19
critical geographies 14
cultural turn 7–9

Dalits 26, 31n28, 33–34, 37, 41, 47, 49, 52, 57, 78, 103, 157, 164; Dalit Bahujan 119, 122n20; #DalitLivesMatter 57; #DalitWomenFight 57; *58*
Darwin, Charles 81
Datta, Ayona 89
decolonising geography 13–15, 72
Decolonising the Mind (Thiong'o) 12
Del Casino, V. J. 4
Delhi 27, 48–49, 89
Denmark: citizenship and belonging in 98–101; protest against Niqab/Burqa ban in *100*, 100–101

Detroit Geographical Expedition Institute 70–72
difference 28–29, 162, 164–165; geographies of 63–68, 93–94; creating knowledge 68–74; *see also* bodies; citizenship and belonging; gated communities; identities; intersectionality; mobility and immobility; more-than-human geographies; precarity
digital economy 109
digital labour 108–113, 120
digital platforms 109–113
digital technology 108–112; *see also* gig economies
disabled people 19, 128, 140–142
disabling environments 140–142, 148
domestication 82

Egypt *35*, 36, 112
8th amendment 42–45
environment 5–6, 19–20; environmental determinism 8, 11–12, 19, 22, 166; environmental movements/activists/protests 34, 39–40, 49
European Commission 107
European Union (EU) 78, 85, 106, 144; Fortress Europe 78
everyday life 125, 130, 133
exclusion 75

Fairwork 112
fake news 73, 74
Floyd, George 55–56
Foreigners Tribunals 102
Forests Rights Act 2006 38
Foucault, M. 25
Four Fights campaign 93

gated communities 74–80, 77, *79*, 90, 164; *see also* in place/out of place
geographic scale 20
geographers, accidental 155–161
geography: animal 81–83; decolonising 72–73; discipline

186 INDEX

of 68, 72–73; hybrid 82; of inclusion/exclusion 75; more-than-human 8, 80, 90
Ghana 112
gig economies 103–104, 110–113, *111*, 120
globalization of corporations 103–105; Ireland's state tax 105–108, 120; *see also* digital platform; gig economy; good life; labour and paid employment
Global North 64, 105, 117
Global South 28, 84, 105, 137
good life 113–114 *see* livable lives
Grace Banu 118–120
Gramsci, Antonio 24
Green Revolution 46–47
Guangzhou 129, 132–133
gurrutu 18

Hägerstrand, Torsten 17
Halappanavar, Savita 42–43, 45
Hamad Port 137
Haraway, Donna 81
Harvey, David 6–7, 17
hegemony 24
Henley Passport Index 144
hierarchies of belonging, India 101–103
Hijras 116, 118
hukou 129–130
human/non-human relationships 82–83
hybrid geographies 82

identities 25–27, 63–65, 116, 162; *see also* belonging; bodies
immobility 125–128, 149; *see also* mobility
immigration policies 78, 101
inclusion/exclusion, geographies of 75
India: hierarchies of belonging in 101–103; Niyamgiri protests 36–41; protests against NRC laws (new citizenship laws) in

101–103; resource colonialism 10; smart cities 89; trans activism in 118–120
Indian Farmers' Protests: Dalit community 49–50; farming system 48; Green Revolution 46–47
Indigenous communities 37, 39–41, 69
in place/out of place 75
international division of reproductive labour 146–147
intersectionality 64–65
invasion 77
Ireland 42; access to housing 108; disabled people in 142; healthcare in 45, 107; marriage bar 42; Repeal activism in 41–45; settler colonialism 10; tax status 105–108; *see also* abortion, Ireland

Jantar Mantar 116
jus sanguinis 98
jus soli 97

Kaepernick, Colin 53–54
kafala 136
Kerketta, Jacinta 38
knowledge 68–70; creating 68; official and hierarchical 70
Kropotkin, Pyotr 55

labour and paid employment 104
Lee, Robert E. 56
Lefebvre, Henri 16
left-behind children 131
LGBTQI+ people 114–118; mobility of 138–139; *see also* trans activism, India
liberal democracies 99–101
liveable lives 113–120; and precarity 95–96; Pride (LGBTQI+ people) 114–117; transgender community 118–120; *see also* good life
Live-In Caregiver Programme (LCP) 146–147
Livingstone, David 68

Majhi, Bhagwan 37–38
Māori 18
Marxism 6–7, 9, 16; Marx, Karl 7
materialities 76, 84
Mbembe, Achille 95
Merriman, Peter 17
migrants 128; care work and hierarchies of 145–148; in China 129–134; Filipina 146–147; highly skilled 78, 144; internal, in India 126–128; South American 142–143; workers, in Qatar 136–137
migration 21, 124–128, 148–149; care work 146–147; circular 130; 3D jobs 130–131; of highly skilled workers 144–148; *hukou* system 129; internal, in China 128–134; left-behind women 131; in Qatar 136–137; remittances 132
Milk Co-operative Society 118–120; *see also* Grace Banu
mobile methods 134, 135
mobilities turn/new mobilities paradigm 125–126, 134, 139
mobility 125–128, 148–149: borders and 142–144; disability and 139–142; gating in EU 78; and immobility 125–126, 128, 139, 141, 148–149; nationality and, rights 144–145; politics of 145–148; relationship between, and space (case of Qatar) 135–139; *see also* migrants; migration
mobility justice 139, 147–148
Modern Geographical Thought (Peet) 7
more-than-human geographies 8, 80, 90
movement 21, 149; *see also* migrants; migration; mobility; mobility and immobility
Movement for Black Lives (M4BL) 52–53
Muslim women 100–101

National Crime Records Bureau 2019 47
National Geographic (magazine) 69
National Population Register (NPR) 101
National Register of Citizens (NRC) and protests in India 101–103
naturalised citizenship 98
nature-culture/hybrid geographies 82
necropolitics 95
neocolonialism 12
neoliberalism 104–106, 120
networks 23; of solidarity 57; transnational 39, 105
Ngũgĩ wa Thiong'o 12–13
Niyamgiri protests 36–41
non-governmental organisations (NGOs) 39–40

online protests 53; *see also* social media
orientalism 70
Orissa 36–39; bauxite deposits 36–37; Niyamgiri protests in 36–41
othering 26, 90, 94

Paddington (film) 69
paid employment 104–105
Pain, R. 3
Panelli, R. 3
Parreñas, Rhacel 146–147
Peet, Richard 7–9, 11
politics of movement *see* mobility
post-humanism 81
post-truth landscapes 73–74
Poulsen, Soren Pape 99
power 24–25
praxis 14–15
precariousness 92
precarity 92–96; and difference 94; livable life and 95–96; necropolitics 95; *see also* citizenship and belonging; globalization of corporations; digital labour; gig economies; hierarchies of belonging, India; labour and paid employment

188 INDEX

pregnancy 42
pride: Delhi Queer Pride 115–116, *115*; *see also* LGBTQI+ people
proletariat 21
protests 49; *see also* Arab Spring; #BlackLivesMatter; Indian Farmers' Protests; India, protest against Niqab/Burqa ban; Niyamgiri protests; National Register of Citizens (NRC) and protests in India; online protests

Qatar World Cup, mobilities turn 128, 134–139
Queensland government 41
queer geographies 14
queer people 26, 103, 114, 145
queer time 18

Ratzel, Friedrich 5–6, 11–12
Reclus, Élisée 5–6
Rees, Marvin 56
refugees 99, 101–102, 143–144
relations 22–23
remittances 132
research methods 134–135
resistance 24, 33–36, 47; of Indigenous communities 41; *see also* protests
resource colonialism 10
Roe v Wade Supreme Court 42; *see also* abortion, Ireland
Royal African Company (RAC) 56
Royal Geographical Society (RGS) 68–69, 72

Said, Edward 69–71
Sandeep Nagar 119; *see also* Grace Banu; Milk Co-operative Society
scale 20–23
Semple, Ellen Churchill 11–12
settler colonialism 10
sex/sexuality 42, 45, 114, 118, 144–145

smart cities 86–89; Germany smart city technologies 89; UK smart cities 89; *see also* resource colonialism
smart technologies 87
Smith, Neil 20
social and cultural geography 7–8, 156, 161
social change *see* activism; communities; protests; resistance; solidarity
social geographers, main interests 26–27; *see also* geographers, accidental
Social Justice and the City (Harvey) 6
social lives 2, 15, 20, 23, 27, 149
social media: Arab Spring 35–36; #BlackLivesMatter 52–53, 55; hashtags 57, *58*; collecting/ donating supplies during Covid-19 via 59; India's Farmer Protests 50; Repeal campaign in Ireland 44; post-truth 74; *see also* digital labour
social movements 6, 24, 26–27, 34, 47–48, 52, 54–55, 57; *see also* activism; protests; resistance; solidarities
social reproduction 112, 145; *see also* care work; women
solidarities 35–36, 43–44, 52–58
space 16; social space 16, 83, 140, 157, 162–163, 171; spatiality 16
sports-washing 138
starchitecture 137
Supreme Court of India 38, 40, 118, 167

tax *see* globalization of corporations, Irelands' state tax
Taylor, Thomas Griffith 12
technologies 83–84, 86–89
Temporary Protection Directive 143
3D jobs 130–131

INDEX 189

time geography 17
time-space convergence 22
trans activism, India 118–120
transgender 102–103, 118–120
Trump, Donald 53, 142

UK Supreme Court 98
University and College Union
  (UCU) 93
Utkal Aluminium International
  Limited company 37

Vedanta Corporation 38–40, 119;
  see also Niyamgiri protests
vegetarian diet 82
Vidal de la Blache, Paul 5–6

walled communities *see* gated
  communities
Warren, Gwendolyn 70
welfare states 105
women: Black 52, 64–65; care work
  and 145–148; #DalitWomenFight
  57–58, *58*; Filipina 146–147; left-
  behind 131–132; marginalized, in
  smart cities 89; Muslim 100–102;
  private *vs.* public spaces 26; protest
  against Niqab/Burqa ban in India
  100, 100–101; and sexuality 42–43;
  social reproduction 145–147; trans
  119–120, *120*; *see also* abortion

Zimmerman, George 52

Taylor & Francis eBooks

www.taylorfrancis.com

A single destination for eBooks from Taylor & Francis with increased functionality and an improved user experience to meet the needs of our customers.

90,000+ eBooks of award-winning academic content in Humanities, Social Science, Science, Technology, Engineering, and Medical written by a global network of editors and authors.

TAYLOR & FRANCIS EBOOKS OFFERS:

- A streamlined experience for our library customers
- A single point of discovery for all of our eBook content
- Improved search and discovery of content at both book and chapter level

REQUEST A FREE TRIAL
support@taylorfrancis.com

Printed in the United States
by Baker & Taylor Publisher Services